PORSCHE RACING

PORSCHE RACING

DAVID & ANDREA SPARROW

ACKNOWLEDGEMENTS

The author and publishers would like to express their grateful thanks to Porsche AG Zuffenhausen and Weissach, to the Porsche Museum and to Porsche GB Ltd, in particular Press Manager James Pillar. All have opened their archives to provide photographs and information and given generously of their time to answer queries.

Additional information was kindly supplied by James McCarter. Author and journalist Mike Cotton – surely one of the best known Porsche commentators around – graciously corrected some of the worst howlers and added his thoughts on GT1, Weissach and racing in North America.

Pictures on page 50 (t) and 74 by John S Allen; page 84, Chris Harvey; pages 6, 97, Andrew Morland; pages 98-99, Rothmans; and pages 70 (t), 130 (b), 131 (t), 157, Sutton Photographic. All other images are either from Porsche archives or by David Sparrow.

First published in Great Britain in 1997 by Osprey,
a division of Reed Books, Michelin House,
81 Fulham Road, London SW3 6RB
and Auckland, Melbourne

ISBN 1 85532 616 7

Managing Editor: Shaun Barrington
Editor: James McCarter
Design: the Black Spot

Printed in China

*For a free catalogue of all books published by
Osprey Automotive please write to:*
Osprey Marketing, Reed Books, Michelin House,
81 Fulham Road, London, England SW3 6RB

HALF TITLE **Udo Schutz drives his 2000cc 6 cylinder Porsche prototype to overall victory in the 1000km race at the Nürburgring on 28th May 1967. His co-driver in the race was Joe Buzzetta from the USA**

TITLE PAGE **"The first thing is that we are a bit faster than the McLaren, which helps." (Thierry Boutsen on the GT1, Le Mans 1996). Roll cage as integral chassis member, 100 litre safety fuel tank with integrated catch tank, TAG 3.8 engine management. Apart from a few changes to the transmission etc, it's just like the GT1 road version ... Actually, the road car really *isn't* that far off – 190mph and 0-62 in 3.7 seconds, 544 bhp at 7000 rpm, plays 600 bhp at 7200 rpm**

CONTENTS

INTRODUCTION

PREVIOUS PAGE
A Porsche 906 taking
part in the Targa Florio.
From 1956 through to
1973, Porsche cars
notched up
a string of impressive
overall and class
victories in this
demanding race

There is usually some defining point when the Porsche bug takes hold and the enthusiast realizes that he or she is going to spend a great part of the rest of their lives thinking about Porsches. The compulsion may take the form of the quest for road car ownership or participation in racing itself, or simply buying the magazines, books and videos. Porsche have produced some of the defining sports cars in motoring history, cars that have dominated both the market and the racetrack. The Porsche enthusiast is aware of that history, and we hope that this volume provides at the very least a visual reminder of former and contemporary glories.

For some, Porsche racing memories stretch back to the classic days of the 1950s and models like the 356 and the 550 in hillclimbs and races such as the Mille Miglia. Others have grown up with the Porsche 911, watching its development and refinement over thirty years of production and competition since it was first introduced in 1963. Just a few months after the very first 911 came off the production line, one was competing in the Monte Carlo Rally, coming home fifth, hot on the heels of the 'real' competition 904! That undefined gradation from the genuine privateer through the works-supported entrant to the out-and-out works racer, which has always marked Porsche in competition, is very much part of the allure.

It is a confusion paralleled by, for example, the constant rule changes at Le Mans: what is

RIGHT The annual
Porsche Cup races are
always hard-fought and
never fail to provide
excitement and
entertainment for
spectators. Here 1996
Porsche Cup winner
Bruno Eichmann drives
to victory in the
Porsche 911 GT2

LEFT **A Porsche 924 in racing guise. Porsche has made a commitment to single marque/single model racing, a form of motorsport that has increased greatly in popularity over the past few years**

FOLLOWING PAGES
The Porsche 906 Carrera 6. Porsche expected great things from the car, and it soon started to perform, securing 4th through 7th places at Le Mans in 1966

Le Mans for? Is it a race for slightly modified road cars, designed to let the major manufacturers showcase their latest production models? Or is it in effect an endurance Grand Prix? Whatever the rules have suggested to be the prevailing attitude, Porsche have been equal to the challenge for decades.

During the 1970s, Porsche began to make their presence felt in endurance races around the world, piling up an impressive record of World Championship victories. There were a host of GT victories in Europe by the 911 in its 935 evolution: Le Mans, Spa, Monza, Imola, Nürburgring and many others. The decade also saw the association of the Porsche name with those of Jacky Ickx, Derek Bell, Al Holbert and Hans Stuck, all great partnerships.

Le Mans fans will remember the 1980s as a decade of almost total domination, with other marques seemingly just making up the numbers until Jaguar finally found a way of breaking Porsche's grip on endurance racing. The spectacle of Porsches clocking some 230 mph along the Mulsanne straight was one of the most memorable, awe-inspiring and terrifying experiences, surely one to match any other in motorsport.

It should not be forgotten however that Porsche battled away at the Sarthe circuit for seventeen years with cars that quite simply didn't have big enough engines, before gaining the ultimate prize.

The Porsche racing story also includes the company's forays into the Grand Prix arena and its successes at rallying (including the gruelling Paris-Dakar), the latter a book in its own right of course, but we can pick out a few of the highlights. Perhaps the true fascination of the Porsche marque is that it has always been a model designed to perform to the highest level, living on the edge of what is technically possible. But this has not been achieved at the expense of ultra-exclusivity. For most people, to dream of owning a Ferrari is just that – a dream. But a Porsche is a realizable ambition for far more people.

This book begins with a brief résumé of the early career of Dr Ferdinand Porsche and then follows the company's fortunes in competition up to the present day. Almost alone among manufacturers, Porsche have retained a company philosophy and approach to their product and its competitive programme that can be seen as integral to the company from its earliest days. The stars of the story are Porsche's engineering team, the cars they have produced and the drivers who have explored their capabilities to the limit.

THE BIRTH OF A RACING TRADITION

Environmentalists today look to the electric car as the cleaner future of the automobile. Dr Ferdinand Porsche got there well before them. Perhaps one of the stranger milestones in motor racing happened on September 23, 1900, at Semmering in Austria. This was when the name of Porsche first entered into the record books, as Ferdinand Porsche drove an electric Lohner car of his own design to victory in the hill climb held on the mountain road. His average speed of over 25 mph smashed the existing figure by a margin of more than 30 per cent. Porsche had earlier been appointed chief designer for the company, who were experiencing difficulty in producing a reliable vehicle to market. Porsche's solution was simple and elegant – to fit individual electric motors to the hub of each front wheel. Additional refinement led to a decrease in battery weight and the consequent increase in speed and efficiency.

Ferdinand moved to Austro-Daimler in 1906, which offered greater scope for his racing interests, replacing Paul Daimler as technical director. He competed personally in Austro-Daimlers of his own design up until the beginning of World War 1 in hill climbs and trials. This mixture of hands-on racing experience and technological expertise helped strengthen his conviction that progress was best achieved, and innovations best tested, in competition. 'Racing improves the breed' has been the Porsche credo more obviously down through the decades than for Aston Martin, Jaguar, Ferrari, or any of the great competition marques.

The company began to flourish under the influence of Porsche's enthusiasm. One of his first commissions at the company was to work on the Austro-Daimler Maja, a racing car built for Emil Jellinek, and named after one his daughters. Jellinek was a leading light at the company, and embodied the entrepreneurial spirit of early motoring. He was an avid driver, racing under the pseudonym "Monsieur Mercedes", taking the name of another daughter. Three cars were produced and entered in a Trials race in 1909, but without success.

LEFT The first of so many Porsche records; Ferdinand Porsche at the helm of the Lohner Porsche after his record-breaking drive at Semmering in Austria. It was a decisive victory – Porsche's electric car cutting a third off the record time

Perhaps it was memories of 1900, but Porsche returned to the Semmering hillclimb and duly gained victory there on September 19. However, that date has a more important claim in the Porsche story, for it was on the same day that Porsche's wife gave birth to a son, Ferdinand Porsche Jnr. – Ferry Porsche.

The following year, 1910, Porsche's engineering skills met with greater success, with the 27/80 model, developed for trials. These had 5.7 litre engines developing 95hp which owed much to Austro-Daimler's work with aero engines. Although powerful machines, they were lighter and more aerodynamic than their rivals of the day. Eight cars were entered in the trials and three finished in the top three places, with Ferdinand himself leading the way to win the event.

This was the end of the first chapter in Porsche's life. The build up to the war grew ever more ominous and its effects would change the face of Europe and of course its industry. At the outbreak of World War 1, Ferdinand had just passed his 39th birthday.

He had come a long way since working as a teenage boy in his father's tinsmiths in the village of Maffersdorff, Austria, while studying in the evenings at the local technical college. He was an energetic and ambitious man and had made his mark. Yet if his career had ended here, he would have been no more than one of the more interesting pioneers of the fledgling automotive industry. The Porsche legend as such was still in the making.

LEFT The steady gaze of a genius. When he was 15, in 1890, Ferdinand Porsche built an entire electrical system, including a generator and control board, for his father's house and workshop. His father, who disapproved of Ferdinand's interest in the new magic of electricity, (there was no supply in their Bohemian village) was forced to relent and sent him off to study in Vienna

THE INTER-WAR YEARS

y the time peace was restored, the shape of Europe had been changed for ever. Dr Porsche – in 1916 he had been awarded an honorary doctorate from Vienna University for his achievements – found himself now managing director of Austro-Daimler. He knew that no company could survive in this new post-war environment without a radical rethink. He felt that the days of the huge, extravagant, coachbuilt automobile were over for ever and the age of the smaller car had arrived. But Porsche never really persuaded his more reactionary colleagues at Austro-Daimler of this fact.

In 1921, Porsche was commissioned to design the 'Sascha' – a small, lightweight 1000cc two-seater that could reach 90mph – for Count Sascha Kolowrat, head of Austria's largest film company. Saschas were entered in the Targa Florio that year and finished first and second in their class, with another, slightly modified Sascha seventh. Porsche then set to work on a 2000cc version of the Sascha for the following year, which developed a top speed of over 100mph. Yet despite the Sascha's suc-

cesses, its potential, and the obvious racing precedents that were being set by smaller cars, Austro-Daimler decided to pull out of racing altogether. It it was time to move on once again and Porsche took a new post was as technical director at Daimler in Stuttgart.

Once again his first task was the redesign of an existing engine – a 2000cc supercharged unit which was intended for racing but which had yet to achieve any success. By 1924 the Porsche touch had worked its magic and the vehicle took first, second and third in the Targa Florio, with an outright win for Christian Werner. In the same year Dr Porsche received his second honorary doctorate, this time from the University of Stuttgart.

At the end of the War, Daimler Motoren-Gesellschaft and Benz & Cie had come to an unofficial arrangement to work together. This co-operation helped both companies to survive the severe economic conditions of the early 1920s as profitable concerns. In 1926 they joined officially in a well-planned merger, to create a strong, healthy company, ready to take advantage of the economic upturn when

it eventually arrived. Porsche's stay at Daimler-Benz/Mercedes was to last a relatively short time, but it resulted in one of the most famous cars produced by Dr Ferdinand – the SSK, one of the best-known and loved Mercedes ever, and a true classic.

These huge 6-cylinder cars with their impressive exterior plumbing notched up a whole catalogue of wins. Two drivers in particular played major roles – Rudi Caracciola and Hans Stuck, who were admirably supported by Team Manager Alfred Neubauer. However, despite their successes, Mercedes-Benz as a company never seemed wholly committed to competition. Road cars were seen as the raison d'etre and motorsport wins were simply a vicarious public relations bonus. Yet despite producing no specially-designed racers for almost a decade, Mercedes stayed at the forefront of racing success with the Porsche-designed units, which

says a great deal for the expertise and enterprise of Porsche and his associates, in what must have been a frustrating environment.

Most of their victories came in sports car racing and hill-climb events. In 1930, Stuck won the European Mountain Championship for racing cars and Caracciola the equivalent race for sportscars: the string of successes looked set to continue. Unfortunately, the economic climate was worsening, and as recession turned into full-scale depression the company decided in 1932 to withdraw from racing altogether. Even so, Neubauer ensured that two Mercedes were entered privately that year in the race at Avus and to good effect: Stuck set the lap record of 125mph, but victory went to newcomer von Brauchitsch in an SSKL with a streamlined bodyshape.

Earlier, the short-wheelbased SSK had two outings at Le Mans. Caracciola and Werner in

1930 put everything into the cause, breaking the lap record before being forced to retire with mechanical problems. The following year, Stoffel and Ivanowsky were more fortunate and took second place. Caracciola had previously been victorious in the German Grand Prix of 1926 and the Irish Grand Prix of 1930, becoming in the same year the first non-Italian to win the Mille Miglia.

While the huge and successful Mercedes cars were destined to win every plaudit in sight, Porsche still had his small car in mind. His Daimler colleagues had been supportive, but he found those of the Benz pedigree much less forward-thinking. When his small-car project was shelved in early 1929, Porsche resigned on the spot. He returned to his native Austria to work for Steyr, developing several highly thought-of and commercially successful vehicles there. But this was not to be a long-term relationship. The

bank which owned a major share of Steyr collapsed. Fortunately for the company this bank was rescued by another. Unfortunately for Porsche, this second bank controlled Austro-Daimler, and a merger between the two companies looked inevitable. Porsche did not relish re-establishing a relationship with the company he had left seven years previously. The answer seemed clear: go it alone.

Porsche's position was a strong one from which to embark on such a course. The young man whose formal education had been sparse, who had been obliged to sneak into university lectures uninvited, and who had worked his way up from the bottom of the ladder was now a designer and engineer of renown, with two honorary doctorates to his credit. He had first-rate contacts in the business, and was confident of being able to put together a first-class team. In addition, he had a supportive family, and his son Ferry, now twenty years old, was already turning into an accomplished engineer himself. It was time to make the leap, and the company 'Konstruktionsburo für Motoren- und Fahrzeugbau Dr. Ing. h.c. Ferdinand Porsche, GmbH' was formed on 1st December 1930.

It had long been one of Porsche's enduring dreams to build a good, small car for the average man and his family, a dream that was eventually to be realised as the Volkswagen. But there were false starts and disappointments en route, for these were turbulent times in the automotive industry as elsewhere. Many companies seemed to be in a constant state of flux: mergers, diversifications, refinancings, splits and yet more mergers were the order of the day. One of Porsche's earliest customers was Wanderer, for whom he conceived a highly successful 1.8 litre smallish car. The satisfied client immediately set Porsche to work on a larger, eight-cylinder version destined for the race track. Then in 1932 Wanderer became

Porsche Type 64 of 1939. Three racing coupés were built for the Berlin-Rome-Berlin race. They were based on the Type 60, using an adapted version of the VW motor and aluminium bodywork. The cars could manage a top speed in the region of 145kmh. The race, planned for September of that year, never took place, because at 04.45 on the first, troops crossed the Polish border; and the Tiger tank, designed by Porsche, became more of a priority than record-breaking coupés

part of the new Auto-Union group, and Porsche found himself facing a whole new set of opportunities – and problems.

Inspired by and, in view of his past associations with them, perhaps somewhat annoyed with, the huge subsidy that Daimler-Benz had just received from government coffers to enhance Germany's racing status, Porsche confronted Chancellor Hitler and demanded a similar level of finance. Initially Hitler was furious; the official line was that a Daimler-Benz car would triumph for Germany on the track.

But Hitler also had a keen personal interest in motoring and motor racing, and when he heard Porsche's technical propositions, presented with such enthusiasm, he changed his mind and authorised the money immediately. History does not record the reaction of the luminaries at Daimler-Benz!

The Wanderer project transmuted into the Auto-Union P-Wagen, another of the great early Porsche innovations, the mid-engined design produced by a small independent company, Hochleistungs Fahrzeubau GmbH,

the P-Wagen at this time; early in 1938 he was killed when his car crashed during one such attempt. The P-Wagens went on to win three further Grand Prix races before the outbreak of war brought motor racing to a halt.

Another project involving Porsche at the time was uncharacteristic and perhaps influenced by Chancellor Hitler's desire for German technological glory. In collaboration with Daimler-Benz, Porsche helped build a car to attempt the land-speed record, the Porsche-Daimler Super Automobil. The driver sat near the front, behind him an inverted 44 litre Daimler-Benz aircraft engine capable of over 3000hp. When war broke out, this monster was on a ship en route to the USA and Salt Lake City. It never ran, and today graces the Daimler-Benz Museum in Stuttgart.

More relevant to the future development of the company, was the work Porsche had put into the development of the Volkswagen. From the start, Porsche had discussed with his team the possibility of producing a small sportscar based on this model designed specifically for the man-in-the-street. There were several setbacks in getting this off the ground: since the German authorities were now involved, permission had to be sought for everything; even someone of Dr Porsche's stature and determination had problems. But by 1938, the team had reached their goal – the Type 114 F-Wagen. Three of these cars were prepared for racing, and became known as the Type 60K10. Porsche then persuaded the relevant authorities that a road race from Berlin to Rome would be a good idea. The race was due to take place in September 1939, and naturally all thoughts of it were forgotten when Hitler invaded Poland. The Porsche company transferred back to Ferdinand's homeland of Austria in the town of Gmünd in 1944, to escape the bombing of Stuttgart.

established in November 1932. Its revolutionary 16-valve engine brought immediate success, with Hans Stuck winning two races in the 1934 Grand Prix season in the Type A, and performing well in the remainder. The following year also saw two Grand Prix victories in the Type B, courtesy of Stuck and new team-mate Bernd Rosemeyer, who went on to win three races in 1936 in the Type C. Next came the 'Eifelrennen' the following year, the most powerful P-Wagen version of them all. Rosemeyer broke many speed records with

BEGINNING AGAIN

The years following the end of the Second World War were a traumatic time for the Porsche family. Both Dr Ferdinand and his son Ferry were interned by the Allies and in 1945, they and Anton Piëch, the husband of Porsche's sister Louise, were arrested by the French authorities, on what were later shown to be false charges. Ferry Porsche was released after six months, but it was not until August 1947 that Dr Porsche and Anton Piëch gained their freedom. In the meantime, Ferry had devoted his energies to revitalising the company, which had survived thanks to the efforts of Louise and Karl Rabe, a close friend and associate of Ferdinand from the company's early days, and a brilliant engineer in his own right.

Ferry Porsche signed a contract with Piero Dusio, the founder and head of the Cisitalia company, whose grand dream had long been to produce the ultimate Grand Prix car. The great Tazio Nuvolari was pencilled in as lead driver. Although this was not an area with which Porsche were most familiar, the design they produced, the Cisitalia-Porsche Type 360, displayed some ground-breaking innovations. It was based on a chrome-molybdenum space-frame chassis and powered by a horizontally-opposed 12 cylinder engine, mounted between the cockpit and the rear axle. The gearbox was a Porsche 5-speed fully synchromeshed unit, fitted to a drive system which allowed the driver to select either rear-wheel or four-wheel drive. This allowed the driver to corner at power using rear wheels only and then pull out with full traction using all four wheels. Suspension was torsion bar springing front and rear. Although the engine was just 1500cc, the car developed an astonishing 385hp thanks to supercharging.

Alas, the Cisitalia was never to be proved in action. Dusio's plan was to have six vehicles taking on all-comers, but the vision began to outrun the costs incurred. By early 1949, creditors were baying for money owed and employees began demanding unpaid wages. A crisis was at hand, and temporary salvation came from an unlikely source – President Peron of Argentina. Peron offered to cover Dusio's debts if he, in turn, would move to Argentina and help develop that country's motor industry. He agreed, and Auto Motores Agentinos – known as Autoar – was formed. The Citalia 360 did make a brief appearance in Italy with Nuvolari at the wheel, but this was for publicity purposes only. In 1950 the car was shipped to Argentina where it lay unused, apart from a brief outing for practice in the Buenos Aires Grand Prix in 1953. Porsche relocated the Cisitalia in 1959 and brought it back for the company museum in Stuttgart. (By September 1950, the company had transferred all activities back to Zuffenhausen, Stuttgart, from Gmünd as the Americans withdrew.)

Perhaps chastened by this experience, and echoing his father's convictions about the future of automobile development, Ferry Porsche's thoughts turned again to a VW-based sports car. The first prototype, to be designated retrospectively the 356/1, was designed by Erwin Komenda and was completed early in 1948. It was to prove a landmark vehicle, taking victory in its class in a road race at Innsbruck in July that year. It was to be the first of many such wins in a line of cars whose design history can be traced back seamlessly to this very first model. This success was followed by the 356/2 which later became known, after a few bodyshape modifications, as simply the 356.

On January 30th, 1950, Dr Ferdinand Porsche died, aged 75. His son Ferry took his place as head of the company. One era had ended and another begun.

Traum
Der
der
Zukunft

LEFT **Composite PR photograph 1948 style to promote the success of the Innsbruck road race. Top right is Otto Mathe in his Berlin-Rome-Berlin Porsche Type 64. Bottom left & right is Herbert Kaes in a Porsche Type 356 Roadster**

The 356 that gave Porsche its landmark first victory in the Innsbruck race of 1948, with Herbert Kaes at the wheel, was to all intents and purposes an unadorned road-car, with a maximum speed of just 84mph. But by the beginning of the new decade, cars were being prepared specially for competition, designated SL. They brought further class successes in the Alpine rally for Mathe and the Swedish Rally for Berckheim, who repeated the win the following year, also driving to victory in the Travemunde rally. There were class wins, too, in the Tour de France for Pickard and Farge, and in the Liège-Rome-Liège Rally a second place for Huschke von Hanstein and Petermax Muller. People were beginning to sit up and take notice, although the company was still not widely known of outside motorsport circles.

Porsche crossed the Atlantic in 1951 and found victory in the USA with the 356s, Cunningham winning a class victory at Palm Beach, and Max Hoffman doing the same in a cabriolet at the Mount Equinox hillclimb in Vermont. Shortly after, Hoffman imported three race-prepared SLs into the USA, but they did not do that well, winning only once, in California, with John von Neumann at the wheel.

The Liège-Rome-Liège outing was successful that year, too, with Helmut Polensky and Walter Schluter winning the rally and five out of the top ten places going to Porsche. Other encouraging results were success in the Mille Miglia for the 1500 of Count Lurani and Konstantin Berckheim, who won their class and finished within the top fifty. Hans Hermann also gained class victory at the Nürburgring. These early successes led Porsche to produce a racing engine, the 528, which was fitted into the 356 and helped that car take first place in the Carrera Panamerican Road Race in Mexico in 1953, where they were pitted against their newly introduced 550 brothers, of which more shortly. In 1954, the Sports Car Club of America held national championships for the first time and the F production honours were shared by Richard Thompson and Art

Bunker, both behind the wheel of production Porsche 1500s. The 1500s established a popular and successful reputation: when they did not actually win they always seemed to put in a good race and demonstrated admirable reliability. They were certainly instrumental in consolodating what was becoming an increasingly enviable competition record for Porsche during the early 1950s; and would be enjoyed by owners and enthusiasts for much longer.

As great a landmark for the company during 1951 was surely Porsche's first entry at Le Mans. The company put up four 356SLs, although two cars didn't make it any further than practice, being virtually written off. The third came to grief early on in the race. It was left to Frenchman Auguste Veuillet and co-driver Edmond Mouche to bring home the honours for Porsche. Driving a 1949 silver Gmünd-built coupé powered by a 1086cc flat-four engine, prepared only by tuning and a little aerodynamic improvement, they finished in a highly respectable overall 20th place, taking first place in the class. This was improved

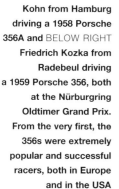

ABOVE RIGHT **Ralph Kohn from Hamburg driving a 1958 Porsche 356A and** BELOW RIGHT **Friedrich Kozka from Radebeul driving a 1959 Porsche 356, both at the Nürburgring Oldtimer Grand Prix. From the very first, the 356s were extremely popular and successful racers, both in Europe and in the USA**

ABOVE **Franz-Josef Berg from Aachen in Germany drives a Porsche 356B from 1960 at the AvD Oldtimer Grand-Prix at the Nürburgring in 1995. The Oldtimer events provide a unique opportunity to see classic racers of every marque in their element**

LEFT **Porsche Type 356 Roadster in Gmünd. At the wheel is Rudolf Ruhrl, who was formerly a member of Hans Stuck's racing team. The Gmünd-built cars started the Porsche company off on the road to post-war success, both in the building of road cars, and on the race track**

ABOVE **Porsche 356B 1960 at the Nürburgring driven by Walter Rosenlechner and M Olsson-Rosenlechner of Sweden. The 356B earned special praise for its superior handling and all-round road hugging ability, regardless of severity of bend or perversity of camber**

ABOVE RIGHT **Porsche 718 RSK from 1958 driven by Wessel Loringhaven from Dusseldorf. The Type 718 replaced the 550A in this year, the K designation indicating a new front suspension system**

RIGHT **Porsche 550A from 1957 with Heinz Schmidt of Neu-Isenburg at the wheel. The car made a name for itself as being virtually indestructible; although the Porsche's 1500cc engine gave 135bhp, there were many more powerful cars on the track – the Porsche won out because it just kept on going**

on the following year, winning class again and finishing overall 11th. A small taste of the huge achievements to come at what many consider the most prestigious event in motor racing.

The Porsche 356 had met with a remarkable degree of success and laid the foundations for the company to pursue its racing ambitions. The Le Mans experience of 1951 led Ferry Porsche to set his engineers the task of building a 356 derivative specifically for racing. The brief was as straightforward as it was ambitious: the mechanics should be simple, light and reliable, and the vehicle fast

enough to win races. The result was unveiled at the Paris Motor Show of 1953, the Porsche Type 550 Spyder. In looks, it was reminiscent of an earlier car, the Glöcker Porsche of 1950. This had been built by racing enthusiast and Frankfurt VW dealer, Walter Glöcker, a stylish open top powered by a modified Porsche 1100 cc engine producing 53hp, mounted just to the front of the rear axle. The Glöcker looked good and didn't disappoint when put to the test, winning the German 1100cc title three years in a row. A second version, fitted with a Porsche 1500 cc unit producing 90hp, with slightly modified styling, the Glöcker-Porsche as it became known was even better.

The Spyder 550 met with a few teething troubles, particularly with the new 1547cc engine that had been designed for it by Dr Ernst Fuhrmann, so a modified form of the 528 unit was employed instead. As a makeshift it performed impressively, winning the 1953 Eiffelrennen at the Nürburgring and taking its class title at Le Mans, where it was clocked at 124 mph down the Mulsanne straight.

Nevertheless, the car needed its dedicated engine, and that engine was crucial to Porsche's future plans. In fact, it was the first Carrera engine, and although developed with racing as its primary aim, the company had certainly not ruled out the possibility of using it for future production models. It was an impressive creation, sporting all manner of technical goodies, including dual overhead cams, hemispherical combustion chambers, dual-plug ignition fired by twin distributers and one-piece connecting rods. On bench test the 1500 cc unit generated 112 hp at 6,400 rpm.

ABOVE & LEFT **It was their ability to go on and on without breaking down that gave the Porsche 550s their good reputation at the endurance races. Their drivers loved them because they could be driven flat out, without the worry of a sudden ignominious exit due to engine failure. They looked superb on the track then, as they still do today**

(The Carrera dynasty begins in 1955. Named after the Carrera Panamerica road races of the mid 1950s, the first model was produced from September 1955 to April 1957, with either a coupé or speedster body. The 1600 GS or GT 1988 cc model followed in 1958, then in 1960 just the competitiion model.)

The engine was finally united with the 550 later in 1953 and brought victory for Hans Stuck in the hillclimb at Freiburg and for Hans Hermann in the Rhineland Cup. The car also took 1st and 2nd places in the 1500 cc class of the Carrera Panamericana, with a 356 coming in eighth.

There were numerous other class wins too and it was clear that the 550 was making a name for itself as an instant classic. The following year saw class wins in the Mille Miglia and at Le Mans. Hermann and Richard von Frankenberg took 2nd and 1st respectively and with Helmut Polensky in a third car, the 550 was 1,2,3 in the Rhineland Cup. By the end of the year any remaining small niggles with the car (designated the 1500RS by Porsche – RS for Rennsport, signifying a racing model) had been well and truly ironed out. The list of 1955 wins – Sebring, Mille Miglia, Le Mans, Berlin GP, Rhineland Cup – makes the point as clearly as anything else.

The 1500RS had struck a chord with enthusiasts worldwide, but the mid-1950s was a period in which automobile development and the competitiion between rival companies began to accelerate. Porsche knew that it could not rest on its laurels and that competition would only getter tougher. In 1956 the 550 was updated and refined to become the 550A, with stiffer frame, new suspension and gearbox and larger brakes. Before long, this model earned itself a reputation as being almost unbreakable, whatever stresses and torques it was subjected to.

The first wins came almost immediately: Umberto Maglioli stormed to a decisive victory in the Targa Florio, and the model won most of the endurance races in which it was entered, both in 1956 and the following year, on both sides of the Atlantic. It was an elegant, responsive machine, light and nimble in the drive. It could withstand far more punishment when cornering than its heavier rivals and also had the reliability which was becoming a Porsche trademark, able to race hour after hour without suffering brake, clutch or engine failure.

Development continued apace. In 1958 Porsche introduced yet another new racer, designated the RSK 718/1500 and known as the RSK1500. With better rear suspension and more power than its predecessors it proved

Porsche 718 RSK from 1958 with Dr Klaus Racker at the wheel. In that year driver Jean Behra drove a 1500cc-engined RSK to victory in the Rheims Formula 2 race, beating off stiff competition which might have been expected to outperform it. Porsche's reputation for outstanding, race-winning cars was growing fast

both popular and adaptable. As well as the by now almost expected class wins at Sebring, the Nürburgring 1000 kms and Rheims, it took the SCCA F sports racing and F production car championships, plus the European Mountain Championships, appearing there in its BergSpyder (mountain-spyder) form. The same year saw Jean Behra modify his 2-seater SSK into a single-seater form and thrash the opposition in the Rheims Formula 2 race.

In 1959, there was a power boost and the car made a debut run in the Formula 2 at Monte Carlo. Not such a good start this time, as Wolfgang von Trips crashed on the very first lap. Compensation came, however, in the Targa Florio, with the RSK, RS and two Carreras filling the first four places, in that order. Porsche's hillclimbing tradition was upheld too, the marque filling places one to five. Across the water, the SCCA Championships again went to Porsche and the endurance race honours were heavily in their favour, too. The remarkable 1500 cars had consistently matched competitors with capacities twice their size, taking third in the world sportscar championships in both 1958 and 1959.

In 1960, Porsche decided to change the car's designation to the RS60, and for the following year it became the RS61. The abstruse logic of company designations apart, the truth is the Spyder program had reached its culmination and was beginning to be run down, partly in anticipation of likely changes to come

in international motorsport regulations for 1962. Despite this, the new RS's continued to compete and notched up class and rally wins to emulate the successes of the RSK 718s.

Although the Carreras had won almost everything going in the late fifties, Porsche never forgot that there were challenges on the horizon from other manufacturers, challenges they met by continued evolution and innovation. They commissioned twenty lightweight aluminium bodies from the firm of Scaglione, which was associated with the designer Carlo Abarth, and so these cars, which were powered by the 1600 Carrera engine from the 356, became known as the Abarth-Carrera GTLs. (Only 18 were actually built.) These cars weighed just 1711 lbs (778 kg) compared to

LEFT **The Carrera GTL Abarth grew out of Porsche's desire to meet the challenges that the other manufacturers were providing. They commissioned twenty lightweight bodies to be built by Abarth in Italy (though it would appear that the work was actually carried out by Zagato). Constructed from aluminium, they were fitted with only the bare essentials by way of appointment, with plastic side windows held closed with crude leather straps**

BELOW LEFT **The Porsche RS60 from 1960. While aesthetic considerations were not a high priority, the Spyders are very pretty to look at, especially in motion on the track**

FAR LEFT **Porsche RS60 from 1960. Building the Spyders was a painstaking and highly skilled task; preparing them for racing was equally skilled of course, and maximising their potential was surely a marriage of art and science**

LEFT **Porsche on the track; every track different, and the trick being to come up trumps at as many of them as possible! This was a skill that Porsche had fine-tuned over the years, and they were now masters of the game**

BELOW LEFT **The Porsche RS61 appeared in 1961, not unreasonably, to replace the RS60. It had a longer wheelbase than its predecessor, and larger wheels. The Spyders always attracted a crowd in their racing heyday, and they still do so today**

2024 lbs (920 kg) for the 356B. There were a few initial problems to sort out, but in 1960 the car made its debut. The body had no bumpers, flush door handles and an adjustable air scoop on the louvred engine lid. It is a little difficult to decide just how much input Carlo Abarth actually had. It seems that the bodies were actually built by Zagato, but that company's involvement with Porsche's competitors made the work a little sensitive, so Abarth became a middleman, fitting bodies to chassis. The Carrera GTL Abarth was first in its class at the Targa Florio, Sebring and Le Mans, and took the first three class places at the Nürburgring. There was a new 1966 cc engine fitted for the 1962 season in the Carrera 2000 GS, and the successes followed a similar pattern to the previous year, with the addition of a class win at the Paris 1000 km race. In 1963 there was a first/second/third in class at Daytona to celebrate.

But this was also a period in which there were longer term considerations at stake. Porsche as a company may have retained a sense of continuity between its various models, but it had also been ready to make a quantum leap forward when it became obvious to engineers that new technologies required new applications. 1964 saw the construction of the 904 or Carrera GTS, not based upon a production car but utilizing a box girder frame with fibreglass body and fully independent suspension; the association with Abarth was over. The 1950s was an astonishing decade for Porsche, establishing itself as one of the great racing marques, one which had an identity which was uniquely its own. Yet these were still the company's adolescent years – the 1960s brought new challenges which Porsche accepted with its customary enthusiasm and ingenuity, building on the strength of achievements to date.

CHAPTER THREE

THE MIGHTY 900s

PREVIOUS PAGE
The Porsche 956s which
dominated Le Mans in
1982. Numbered one,
two and three, they
came home 1, 2, 3

BELOW The 1963
Porsche 904 Carrera
GTS was a new
beginning. The car was
immediately successful,
taking the first two
places in the Targa Florio
in 1964, and coming
towards the front of the
field in the season's
endurance races, with
five 904s finishing in the
top 12 at Le Mans

Tracing the evolution of Porsche models from the early 1960s onwards is made the more difficult by the company's idiosyncratic method of designating each type it produced. Cars are given model numbers which do not necessarily follow in consecutive numerical order – the 907, for example, was introduced after the 910. This chapter looks at the development of those 900 models which were developed and raced from the early 1960s through to the early 1990s, with the exception of cars belonging to the astonishing 911 series, which are described separately in chapter 4.

In 1962 work began on Porsche's new car, the 904. This was the first of a new breed of racing car which owed less to Porsche's experience with production models and much more to pure racing technology, sharing certain design elements with the Formula 1 car (see chapter 7). The bodywork to the rear was of one piece and lifted up on rear hinges for ease of mid-race adjustments. International motorsport regulations required that 100 cars be built for homologation, and Porsche completed the quota in time for the start of the 1964 season. The 904 Carrera GTS was usually fitted with the tried and tested 4-cylinder engine in

LEFT **This Porsche 904 from 1964 is one of 100 built to qualify the car for racing – in fact only these 100 were ever built, even though, with top speeds of over 260kmh (160mph) and a 0 to 100kmh (60mph) time of around six seconds, the 904 was a very desirable car indeed**

BELOW LEFT **The Porsche 904 Bergspyder; Porsche's racers in Bergspyder form – shortened hillclimbers – won many victories and slashed many records. In 1964, Rossfeld and Mitter did the honours**

2000cc form, but sometimes raced with the six-cylinder from the 911 or a 2200cc version of the 8-cylinder 771 Formula 1 engine. First victory for the 904 was at the Targa Florio, where it gained first and third. This was followed by a third at the Nürburgring 1000 km and five cars in the top 12 at Le Mans. The following year class wins included Daytona, Monza, the Spa 500 km and the SCCA championships; the renowned driver Eugen Bohringer would also compete for Porsche in the Monte Carlo Rally that year, finishing in overall second place.

1966 saw the debut of the first car to be designed by Ferdinand Piëch, son of Ferry Porsche's sister Louise. This was the 906, also called the Carrera 6. The 906 was the most streamlined racer so far to emerge from the Porsche stable. Its tubular space-frame kept

weight to a minimum, as did the magnesium and aluminium alloys used for the 911 engine, which was otherwise similar in design to the production version. It quickly proved its mettle with an outright win and four in the top ten at the Targa Florio and 4th, 5th, 6th and 7th places at Le Mans. There were successes at Daytona and Sebring too.

A further refinement in 1967 brought the 910/6, which used the same engine as the 906 but had an even lighter bodyweight and an even more aerodynamic bodyshape. Its improved suspension owed much to

Porsche's hillclimbing experiences. Once again there was the 771-inspired 8-cylinder engine as an option, designated the 910/8, which also appeared in Bergspyder form, although it was the six-cylinder cars that were most successful, with good placings at the 1967 Targa Florio, Daytona, Monza and Spa, and the first three placings at the Nürburgring 1000 km.

In 1968 Porsche also produced the 909, which was built specifically as a hillclimb car. Hillclimbing was a natural arena for rear-engined sportscars and Porsche used their

experience here to good effect, trying and testing out lightweight materials and weight-saving designs on the Bergspyders before applying them to longer-distance racing cars. The sixties were a successful time for hillclimbing, with Edgar Barth winning for Porsche in 1959, 1963 and 1964 and Gerhard Mitter in 1966, 1967 and 1968. This last win was not the happy triumph that it should have been, for Mitter's teammate Lodovico Scarfiotti was killed when his car left the road – the first loss of a racing driver for Porsche. After this, Porsche as a company largely abandoned hillclimbs to concentrate on the Manufacturer's Championship, although many enthusiastic privateers still flew the flag.

As the decade came to an end, Porsche racing cars were arriving in quick succession.

ABOVE LEFT **The Porsche 910 took over from the 906 in 1967. It used the same engine as the 904, but there was also an 8 cylinder version available. There were notable successes for the car at Daytona and Sebring, and also in the Nürburgring 1000km**

LEFT **The Porsche 906, or Carrera 6, was the first project to involve Ferdinand Piëch, son of Ferry Porsche's sister, and grandson of Ferdinand Porsche. Initial outings for the car were encouraging, including a laudable 4th, 5th, 6th and 7th at Le Mans in 1966**

The Porsche 909
Bergspyder made its
debut at the Gaisberg
hillclimb, the penultimate
race of the European
Hillclimb Championship
of 1968. The new car had
been endowed with
superior driving qualities.
Especially developed for
hillclimbing, it was made
of light materials,
weighed 430kg, was
fitted with a 1981cc
engine, and was capable
of 250kmh (150mph)

Whenever a new car appeared at the race-track, there were others being developed, designed or conceived. The next major commitment was the 907, originally a special design for Le Mans which featured a particularly sleek bodyshape. It was basically an aerodynamically refined 910, retaining much of that car's chassis and running gear. When introduced in 1967 at Le Mans in long-tail form, the car was powered by the 911 6-cylinder engine. At first the car showed itself somewhat unstable in testing sessions, but it was improved by the time of the race itself and was driven to fifth place overall by Jo Siffert and Hans Hermann. The 907 was the first Porsche competition car to have its steering wheel on the right. The logic of the switch was simple: since most races are driven in a clockwise direction, this seating arrangement was reckoned to give better driver visibility on most corners and provided extra downforce on the inside wheels due to the driver's weight. Good results at hill-climb events led Porsche to fit the 907 with an aluminium tubular space frame in 1968. The engine was replaced by the

RIGHT **The Porsche prototype 907, equipped with 2200cc eight-cylinder injection engine, is driven to victory in the Sebring 12 hour race of 1968 by Josef Siffert and Hans Herrmann**

BELOW RIGHT **The class of '68; Porsche's team of 907s lines up alongside the support vehicle**

2200cc 8 cylinder Type 771 unit. In this version, the car raced to a one-two-three victory in 1968 in the Daytona 24 hour race with drivers Elford and Neerpasch, Siffert and Herrmann, Buzetta and Schlesser. Siffert and Herrmann also won the 12-hour race at Sebring, and Vic Elford ensured a victory in the Targa Florio with a sensational new lap record,

despite losing 17 minutes during a tyre change. All these successes notwithstanding, the Manufacturer's Championship eluded Porsche in 1968, although successes in Sicily and at the Nürburgring brought them the World Cup for Speed and Performance.

Porsche desperately wanted to win that Manufacturers' Championship, and they knew they would have to pull something very special out of the hat to do so. The FIA changed the rules for 1968, introducing a 3-litre limit on the prototype class and also a 5-litre limit on Group 4, which was a category that Porsche had not approached at the time. That special something that Porsche needed turned out to be the 908, basically a 907 with a new, simplified 3000 cc flat 8-cylinder engine based on the 911. One of the early problems that had to be ironed out of the 908 was that of lack of stability. Although a short 908 had won at the Nürburgring, something was definitely amiss. One solution was the fitting of a strut-mounted rear wing with suspension-controlled flaps,

but this didn't have the elegance which characterises Porsche engineering solutions. Everyone at Porsche was concerned – changes had to be made.

Racing manager Huschke von Hanstein relinquished his post after falling out with Ferdinand Piëch; though he continued to work with Porsche in an advisory capacity. Von Hanstein's successor at the helm was Rico Steinemann. His agenda was to make Porsche number one in motorsport, and to achieve it he was going to have to take some radical decisions. Steinemann decided to concentrate on the events that counted. The Championship races. Porsche's reputation was well-enough established in the production car field to leave the rest to the private Porsche drivers, of which there were many – and many of them were very good indeed. He decided to utilise the cars in the best way he could; the spyders for the shorter races, short-tailed coupés for the 'average' races and the long-tailed coupés for the fast circuits. Steinemann also assembled a

LEFT **First outing at Daytona for the prototype Porsche 907 long-tails. With their 2200cc 8 cylinder engine giving 270bhp, the cars were expected to give a good account of themselves, and they did so, taking first, second and third positions**

new driving team; Kurt Ahrens, Jo Siffert, Richard Attwood, Gerard Larrousse, Brian Redman and Bjorn Waldegaard – as formidable a selection as any works team could wish for.

In both coupé and spyder form the 908 brought Porsche the Maker's Championship in 1969 with some spectacular successes along the way: first four places both in the Targa Florio and at the Nürburgring, first and second at Monza. Porsche were edged out of first place at Le Mans, beaten by just 70 metres by a Ford GT40 driven by Jacky Ickx.

While they had been introducing the 908 for the prototype class, Porsche had also been working on a car to take on the best of Group 4; that car was the 917. The 917 chassis was based on that of the 908, but strengthened to accommodate the new engine. This was a real monster,: a 4494cc flat 12 which drew heavily on past experience – both with 908 and with its predecessors. It delivered a heady 580 bhp at 8,400rpm.

So adept had Porsche become at building lightweight cars – and the 917 was very light,

RIGHT **New FIA rules covering prototype-class racing for 1968 made possible the introduction of a new power unit – a 3000cc eight cylinder. This was fitted to the 908 – which from the outside was more or less identical to the 907. This example is a long-tail from 1968**

LEFT The 908 suffered with a multitude of problems, large and small, and looked as if it would never get off the ground. Huschke von Hanstein resigned his post, although he continued to work with Porsche. It was half way through the 1969 season before the 908 started to come good

ABOVE **The Porsche 908 short-tail was renowned for its remarkable manoeuvrability and responsive handling, and performed particularly well on tightly cornered circuits such as the Nürburgring. Porsche never ran the 908s at Le Mans, but privateers did, until rule changes meant ballast, and the 908's key advantage – lightness – was lost. This 908/03, chassis no. 010, has been restored in the Gulf livery worn by Siffert's car at the 1971 Targa Florio**

RIGHT **The Porsche 908 short-tail of 1970 – once successes started to come, they came thick and fast, and the car continued to win races for over a decade**

just above the Group 4 minimum – that they never considered it necessary to engineer any closer to the 5-litre limit. Porsche had got the balance as near perfect as they could.

The regulations put the required number of units that had to be built to qualify at 25, and Porsche already had more 917s than this under construction when they presented the car to the FIA. However, the inspectors ruled that the cars must be completely finished at the deadline and it took an all-out effort on the part of everyone at the workshop to get the job done in time. As before, the car came in short and long-tailed versions to suit the conditions at hand.

The legend of the 917 began at Spa in Belgium in 1969, but its power was such that it took almost a full season to get the car fully balanced and on course for victory. It won the last race of the season that counted towards the Makers' Championship, and led at Le Mans for 20 hours before retiring with gearbox problems. Even so, the car made an impact on those who saw it and it attracted sponsorship for the 1970 season from Gulf-Wyer and Porsche Salzburg. The Martini racing team also entered its first 917 that year, and the cars came into their own with a vengeance. The 917 won everything in sight, with the exception of the Sebring 12 hour race, Targe Florio and Nürburgring, which was won by the special 908/3 model.

More importantly it had brought Porsche's first ever overall win at Le Mans, taking all first three places. No-one minded too much that it

ABOVE LEFT **The Porsche 936. 1976 and 1977 were highly successful years for the car, with a string of victories to its credit**

CENTRE LEFT **Porsche 917 long-tail sporting an attractive livery in which it never raced**

BELOW LEFT **Short-tail Porsche 917 from 1969; not the best year for Porsche in the racing department. Although there were scant victories, the new 917 did put in a good showing towards the end of the season**

was not the specially-prepared long-tailed versions, on which Porsche had spent a great deal of time and effort, which actually came home first: that honour went to a short-tail. The victorious drivers were the veteran driver Hans Hermann, who retired after the race, and Richard Attwood.

The following year the Porsche contingent consisted of three long and three short-tailed 917s, the short-tails bearing the distinctive 'shark fins' on their tails. The competition knew what they had to beat, and Porsche were sure that they would try and match the them. So Porsche increased the capacity of the

ABOVE RIGHT
Le Mans, 1971. The Martini Porsche driven by Marko and van Lennep makes its last stop before claiming class victory. Hellmuth Bott and Klaus Bischof offer encouragement on the right

RIGHT **Gulf-Weyer sponsored a team in 1971 (seen here at Le Mans), just as they had done the previous year, while Martini racing took over the team that had previously raced for Porsche-Salzburg**

engine, first to 4907cc and then to 4998cc. The latter version proved itself best in testing and was chosen to race. But in fact there was very little competition in 1971 – the 917 had frightened off Porsche's rivals, with even Ferrari choosing not to contest the championship that year. Porsches won all the important races; at Daytona, Sebring, Spa, Monza, the Osterreichring and Le Mans, courtesy of the Gulf team and Martini, who had taken over from Porsche Salzburg. Le Mans 1971 was almost an embarrassment: of the 49 cars that lined up on the starting grid, 33 of them were Porsches. The Martini Racing

Team's short-tail, driven by Helmut Marko and Gijs van Lennep, had a surprise in store for the crowd. It used a new magnesium frame in place of the usual aluminium tubular space frame, an astonishing one-third lighter, making the car startlingly fast. A long-tail 917 led the way for the first five hours, but as the half-way point was reached, the Martini short-tail took the initiative, eventually winning by two laps over the second-placed Porsche, and by 31 laps over the third-placed car (a Ferrari). In the 24 hours, they had covered 3,315.2 miles, a record total for Le Mans at that time, at an average speed of 138.13 mph. Porsche again took the World Makers' Championship.

It has often happened that a successful car on a winning streak has been beaten not by a better car coming along but by a change in the rules. This was the fate that befell the 917: it was no longer eligible for the European long-distance races where it had triumphed so resoundingly. So the 917 crossed the Atlantic to embark upon a new career in the Can-Am Championships. These had been started in 1966 by the Sports Car Club of America (SCCA). There were few regulations governing the cars open to entry, other than weight limits, minimum engine capacities and restrictions on the use of aerodynamic encouragement. Porsche developed the 917 engine, boosting the power output first by enlarging it to 5400cc and then employing an Eberspacher turbocharging system. In partnership with Penske racing, who assisted with the development, and with driver Mark Donohue, Porsche took on the Can-Am in 1972. A testing accident put Donohue out of the running, his place being taken by George Follmer, who took the honours that year, storming to victory in round after round. Donohue returned the following year to drive the 917 to victory again.

The 917s were also the car to beat in the

Interserie competition, which they won in 1970 and 1971, and again in 1972 with Leo Kinnunen driving a turbocharged version. It was also a turbocharged version of the 917 which brought victory to Petermax Muller when he won the competition in 1974, a feat he was to repeat in the following year behind the wheel of a turbocharged Porsche 908.

History repeated itself for the 917: a change in the Can-Am rules put them out of the running once more. Perhaps the car was just too good. The 917 did have one last amazing outing – in August 1975, when Donohue set a new lap-speed record at Daytona in a 917/30. The figure was 221.12mph, a record which stood unbeaten for over a decade. This was to be Donohue's last triumph; less than a week later he died at the wheel of his F1 car at the Osterreichring.

LEFT **Rule changes
rendered the 917 a non-
starter for the 1972
season, but the car
crossed the Atlantic for a
new career in Cam-Am
racing. It was necessary
to up the power, which
Porsche, in collaboration
with Penske Racing and
driver Mark Donohue,
accomplished by
turbocharging the 917-10**

BELOW LEFT **Porsche
917 from 1969; the 917
earned a well-deserved
reputation as one of the
Porsche greats**

RIGHT Porsche won all the major races in 1971, including Le Mans, Sebring, Spa and Daytona (pictured), where 917s battled successfully for supremacy

BELOW RIGHT Porsche 917 Can-Am Challenge Cup contender, a hugely powerful car, which was sponsored by Porsche Audi of Teaneck, New Jersey. It was driven in the series by Jo Siffert from Switzerland

The end of the Cam-Am programme signalled a change of direction for Porsche's racing programme. They would now focus their efforts on advanced and innovative versions of the 911 series engine, and that is the subject of the next chapter. However, there were also a number of fascinating models that evolved from Porsche lines independently from the 911 dynasty. For example, in 1976 Porsche decided to make a bid for the new

LEFT The 1973 Can-Am race at Atlanta, totally dominated by Mark Donohue in the impressive 917/30. But regulations were about to interfere again; for 1974 the 917 would be ineligible for the Can-Am series

RIGHT The Porsche 917/30 of the 1973 Can-Am series, the most powerful circuit racing car that had ever been built, with Mark Donohue at the wheel, challenging the established sports racers of Chevrolet, Ferrari and Ford. Exhaust turbocharging had helped create a supercar with 1100bhp

Group 6 class, for which a non-supercharged 3000cc or 2100cc supercharged unit was the order of the day. The designers' answer was the 936, a two-seat streamlined Spyder with a fibreglass body, and the looks of a slightly slimmed-down, modernised Can-Am 917. The engine was a 2142cc turbocharged Carrera RSR which could produce 520hp. Its massive air intake and tail rendered the 936 nothing if not distinctive on the track, and its looks did not belie its performance.

The car quickly distinguished itself as a first-class racer, and took over at Le Mans where the earlier cars had left off, gaining a well-earned victory at the hands of drivers Jacky Ickx and Jochen Mass, plus the World Sports Car Championship.

The car repeated the victory at Le Mans in 1977, with Ickx, Hurley Haywood and Jurgen Barth driving. The 936 sped to its final victory at Le Mans in 1981, with Ickx and Derek Bell at the

wheel, although the second Porsche was plagued by mechanical problems.

In 1982, the international regulations for motor racing changed once again, giving rise to the new sports-racing group C prototypes. At the same time the International Motor Sports Association (IMSA) inaugurated a GT prototype competition for America. Here were two opportunities tailor-made for the type of out-and-out racer at which Porsche excelled, and the resulting cars were the 956 and the 962. The first Group C Porsche, the 956, was

ABOVE LEFT **The victorious Martini Porsche of Ickx and Mass at Le Mans in 1976. The huge air intake dominates the car; the lines of the 936 were very aggressive – but effective**

CENTRE LEFT **First outings for the Martini Porsche 936 in 1976 found it dressed in dark livery, later to be replaced with more familiar white**

BELOW LEFT **In 1977 the Porsche 936 repeated its Le Mans win of the previous year, with victory for the team of Ickx, Hayward and Barth**

powered by a special version of the 935 engine. Group C regulations demanded an increased level of driver protection, a problem which was solved by the used of a light but rigid aluminium chassis and Kevlar panels. Particular attention was paid to aerodynamics, the overall effect being mean and lean. As with Porsche's earlier racers, the 956 was made in both long and short-tailed form.

The car debuted in 1982 and immediately claimed its first Le Mans win for Ickx and Bell, a victory that was to be repeated in 1983. In 1984 Porsche withdrew its works team from Le Mans in protest over hastily-changed regulations, but 956s still stormed home, courtesy of the Joest race team, which repeated the victory in 1985. Porsche took three consecutive International Sports Car crowns in the same period, including a shared championship between old hand Derek Bell and newcomer Hans-Joachim Stuck. However, 1985 was a tragic year for Porsche Motorsport. Two of their drivers were killed on the track: Manfred Winkelhock at Mosport and Stefan Bellof, who had partnered

RIGHT & FAR RIGHT
Porsche's domination in 1982. This was the Le Mans debut for the 956s, and they performed brilliantly. The three cars formed an orderly queue in race order behind car number One, driven by Derek Bell, whose co-driver was once again Jacky Ickx. There have been many memorable Porsche victories, but this was one of the most outstanding, a never-to-be-forgotten experience for everyone who witnessed it

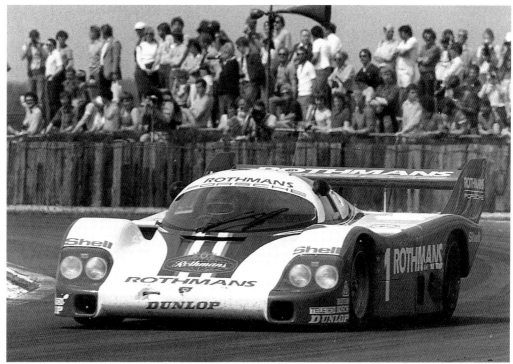

LEFT **Le Mans – 1981.** The 936 driven by Jacky Ickx and Derek Bell cruised to a much-applauded and relatively untroubled victory, while that of Mass, Haywood and Schuppan met one mishap after another, with mechanical niggles and sheer bad luck playing their part. They considered themselves fortunate to finish in overall twelfth place at the end of the day

RIGHT **The famous three – the 1982 Le Mans 956s – in close formation. They crossed the finishing line only a little further apart**

BELOW RIGHT **The winning Porsche 956 on its way to victory in the 51st running of the Le Mans classic. Porsche 956s filled all of the top eight places, while a Porsche 930 Turbo production car won Group B**

Bell at Le Mans and was the reigning World Sportscar Champion, at Spa. It was also a year of disruption and practical difficulties for the team. A refuelling accident at Hockenheim left racing manager Norbert Singer and two mechanics in hospital suffering from burns and shock. In Japan, the skies opened and turned the track into a lethal skid-pad. Team director Peter Falk made the decision to call the Porsches in for everyone's safety.

The 956 was superseded by the 962C, the Group C version of the 962, which carried Derek Bell to his second endurance title in 1986. The 962 also won at Le Mans, with Bell, Al Holbert and Hans Stuck driving. The race though was overshadowed by the death of Jo

LEFT An unusual view of the Rothmans-Porsche 956 of 1982, showing the huge adjustable aerofoil, and giving the car a very 'square' appearance

BELOW LEFT 1982 may have been 'their year', but the 956s continued to win races, giving Porsche three more Le Mans victories, in 1983, '84 and '85, and also the World Championships in the same years

RIGHT **Le Mans 1982;
The victorious Porsche
956 of Derek Bell and
Jacky Ickx in full flight**

BELOW RIGHT **The
Porsche 956s continued
to fight hard and win;
this 956 receives
attention at the
Nürburgring in 1983, a
year in which Porsche
won all seven Endurance
Championship races**

LEFT **The Rothmans Porsche 962C of Jacky Ickx and Jochen Mass storming to victory in the Mugello 1000km race in April 1985. The car was a version of the 962 that Porsche had been developing in the USA for the previous two seasons. Derek Bell and new partner Hans Stuck – son of the Porsche driver of the same name in the 1930s – fared less well in this race; Stuck ran out of fuel on the final lap!**

RIGHT **Mauro Baldi's Ferrari battles with the Konrad Porsche on the banking at Daytona 24 Hours, 3/4 February 1996**

BELOW RIGHT **962, 1989. In that year at Daytona nine 962s were entered and they took first, third and fourth places. (Baldi was co-driver of the one that that did worst!)**

LEFT The Porsche 961 had a short racing career. Appearing for the first time at Le Mans in 1986, the four-wheel drive 961 performed well, coming in in seventh place overall. Thereafter the car performed less well, with major recurring tyre problems. The 961 raced again at Le Mans in 1987, but failed to finish – although this time it was transmission and not tyres that ended its chances

BELOW In 1987, Porsche again added to its tally of outright wins at Le Mans, bringing the total to twelve. Derek Bell, Hans Stuck and Al Holbert formed the team that piloted the 962C to victory

Gartner of Kremer Porsche, the third top driver to lose his life within 12 months. The same team took victory in 1987, although for the other Porsche teams the race was best forgotten, and Bell and Holbert won the Daytona 24 hours. After six years of sponsorship from Rothmans, the 962C took on the red and yellow colours of Dunlop and Shell for 1988, but victory was not to be, Porsche at last losing out to the Jaguar challenge. Although Porsche continued to support the Joest team, this was the end of the chapter for the works teams.

OPPOSITE **The Porsche 962Cs sported new colours for 1988 – the red and yellow of new sponsors Shell and Dunlop. But there was little for either the new sponsors or Porsche themselves to cheer about. There would be no works cars in the following years, although Porsche continued to support Joest Racing's bids for glory**

LEFT **In 1988, Porsche came to the rescue of Richard Lloyd Racing by sponsoring their 962 entry into the Autosport 1000kms race at Silverstone in May. Derek Bell and Tiff Needell took the wheel for the race**

BELOW LEFT **A Richard Lloyd Racing-prepared special Porsche 962C at the Nürburgring in September 1988, with David Hobbs and Martin Donnelly sharing the driving seat**

An American version of the 956, the 962, was now developed. The major differences were that the new car had a longer wheelbase than the 956, to conform to IMSA's rule that the driver's feet must rest behind the front wheel centreline. The tail was different too, and ballast had to be added to bring the car up the the minimum weight to comply with IMSA regulations. It was fitted with an all-air-cooled turbo 911 engine (935) in place of the 956's version which had water-cooled cylinder heads. The 962 made its debut at Daytona in 1984 with father and son team Mario and Mike Andretti driving, but suffered with gearbox overheating problems and failed to finish. Porsche were nevertheless encouraged by this 'test drive' and produced four cars for use by customer teams.

The following year, the 962 was the car to beat. Al Holbert won nine of the 17 races, with Derek Bell as his co-driver on six occasions. The two were first and second in the driver's championship, with Bob Wollek winning at

RIGHT **The 962 which came 'so near but so far' at Le Mans in 1988 for Bell, Stuck and Ludwig. The car was passed on to Kremer racing, who never raced it, but displayed it prominently in their showrooms. The car was then sold on to American Frank Gallogly; the cognoscenti might be able to identify the setting here as Laguna Seca, the light showing off the particularly handsome livery**

Daytona and Sebring. Porsche made their mark on the IMSA Camel GT championship, winning almost everything in sight both in this and the following two years. In 1986 the rules were tightened up, which worked slightly in the opposition's favour, and this made Porsche's triumphs in '86 and '87 even more satisfying. The going was getting tougher by 1988, but in 1989 Bob Wollek and John Andretti were successful in the Miller BF Goodrich 962, winning two races in the IMSA series, and also triumphing at West Palm Beach in the three-hour race. Together with Derek Bell they stormed to victory at Daytona, too. Wollek won for Reinhold Joest at Dijon in the World Championship Series, and, driving with Frank Jelinski, won the first European round of the World Championships in fine style.

Porsche continued to support the racing teams to the hilt, even though they were not entering works teams. In 1990, Joest racing, backed by the Porsche factory, prepared three long-tailed 962s for racing, while Brun and Kremer preferred short-tailed versions, for which they designed new bodywork. Kremer's lead driver, Bernd Schneider was the Porsche Cup champion for the year and one of two Joest Porsches was victorious at Daytona in 1991.

LEFT **One of Joest Racing's two Porsche 962s at Le Mans in 1996. This team, comprising Manuel Reuter, Davy Jones and Alexander Wurz, won the race overall**

BELOW LEFT **At Daytona in 1989, Bob Wollek, John Andretti and Derek Bell were not favourites to win in the 962, but battled hard against the opposition, maintaining a relentless pace that brought them first place**

LEFT **A loophole in the new GT regulations for 1994 gave the perfect opportunity for the Dauer Porsche 962, a rebuilt car based on the road-going version of the 962. Two cars were prepared at Weissach, to be driven by Stuck, Sullivan and Boutsen, and Dalmas, Baldi and Haywood. Everyone was jubilant at their audacious first and third places**

BELOW LEFT, INSET **1992; the team give a toast to ten years of the Porsche 956/962. Left to right; Fritz Spingler (race-engine Master Mechanic), Valentin Schaffer (Chief Engineer), Peter Falk (Race Director), Gerd Schmid (Customer Sport), Helmut Schmid (Engine Technician), Hans Mezger (Engine Designer) , Norbert Singer (Project Director), Horst Reitter (Designer), Eugen Kolb (Body Designer)**

FAR LEFT, INSET **The Joest 962C, prepared in conjunction with Porsche for Le Mans in 1990**

CHAPTER FOUR

THE PEOPLE'S RACER

The 911 holds a special place in the affections of many Porsche followers for a number of reasons. To begin with, it's an old friend, having been in production for over thirty years since its introduction in 1964, without losing its recognisable shape and configuration. It's also probably the finest example of engine evolution on the market, a fact that in itself gives it a cachet and prestige that no other vehicle can match. Add to this its many racing successes on the track, in all types of motor sport, and the fact that the 911 remains competitively priced so that it offers any serious enthusiast a chance to enter the sport at a serious level, and you can see why this model above all inspires such loyalty amongst its followers. In all, over fifty variants of the model have been made, some, admittedly, in very small batches for specific racing purposes, others in large-scale production runs. This chapter traces the development of those models that have made major contributions to the 911's competition pedigree.

Its origins stem from the early 1960s, when it began to become clear to the engineers at Porsche that their trusty old warrior, the 356, had been pushed to the limit of its development. The brief was to find a replacement which would show equal flexibility as a production car and a topline racer. The initial styling on a prototype was carried out by Ferry Porsche's son Butzi. Further refinements took place in another three prototypes, and gradually the shape of what would originally be called the 901 emerged. The wheelbase had been stretched compared to the 356, making it a 2 plus 2 seater with adequate, if limited, luggage space. Engine development centred on a six-cylinder overhead camshaft arrangement equalling the Carrera 2 litre in power output. The original 2 litres decided upon had been chosen and designed with thoughts of

LEFT The four cylinder 912's finest year was undoubtedly 1967, when Zasada won the European Rally Championships, and won outright the Argentine Grand Prix 2000km road race

BELOW LEFT The Porsche 911 in its first sporting event – the 1965 Monte Carlo Rally. Drivers were Linge and Falk, who piloted the new car through some atrocious weather conditions to a class win

RIGHT **Gaban and 'Pedro' driving to an overall win at the Classical Touring Car race at Spa Francorchamps in July 1967 in their Porsche 911 (number 23)**

BELOW RIGHT **Volker Weber from Hamburg drives a Porsche 912 from 1965 at the Oldtimer event. The 912 had a brief but successful racing career**

future increases in mind, perhaps to as much as 2.7 litres, it was thought, should subsequent race track demands require it.

The switch to the new designation, 911, was the result of a complaint from Peugeot, who had laid claim to the 901 designation for production models, so this did not represent any design changes to the vehicle. Almost 11,000 models were made in the first two years, with a further 30,000 912s, which used a modified four-cylinder 356 engine. These baby brothers shouldn't be altogether forgotten, as they appeared creditably in many a rally and road race in the late 1960s. However, it was the 911's impact on the racing scene that was apparent from the start, taking second in the 1965 Targa Florio, beaten only by one of its more powerful Porsche brothers.

In 1967 Porsche set about modifying a 911 to maximise what was then allowed under the rules and regulations and this model was designated the 911R, of which about 20 were built. Weight was drastically reduced by using glass fibre, aluminium and plexiglass where

RIGHT **A rare Porsche 911R at Brands Hatch in 1979; only 23 of these cars were ever made. It first appeared in 1967, and was never homologated for racing, as the Porsche Sales department were unconvinced that they could sell 500. The 911R established five world records at Monza, and performed well in the 24hour race at the Nürburgring**

possible and the race tune meant that the engine could put out 210hp at 8,000 revs. Its first outing was at an endurance test at the Monza circuit, where it set a total of 14 international 2 litre class records, including establishing an average speed of 130.02mph over 20,000 kms. It later turned out that the engine used in the Monza car had, in fact, only recently completed a 100-hour bench test – it was the best Porsche had available in the short time they had. The 911R went on to win the Tour de France outright in 1969. For a while Porsche considered building this version in production numbers that would qualify it for the GT and SCCA races, but the investment involved was considered prohibitive.

In other competitions the standard 911 gave Porsche its first long-awaited in victory in the 1968 Monte Carlo rally, with drivers Vic Elford and David Stone at the wheel and, even better, the second car home was also a Porsche, this driven by the Toivonen and

Tuhkanen pairing. The previous year Alan Johnson drove it to gain GT class wins at Sebring, the SCCA at Daytona and the C class, a title he retained in 1968. The same year saw its almost total domination of the TransAm Series 2-litre class. Rallying became one of the 911's strongholds, with further 1968 victories at the Geneva, East German, Spanish, Swedish and San Remo rallies in the European Championships. A similar tale was told in other areas of motor sport: road races, hillclimbs, endurance races and cross-country rallies. Porsche knew they had created something special and they were quick to develop a whole range of competition specific derivatives to build on their early triumphs.

An obvious option was to expand the capacity of the two-litre engine and attack other class competition – the engine had, after

LEFT & CENTRE LEFT
The Porsche 911R (R stands for Rennsport) was designed by Ferdinand Piech to maximise the rules of rallying. After the success of three test cars, the firm of Bauer was commissioned to produce a run of twenty

BELOW LEFT The Touring Car Championships at the Nürburgring in 1968; this is a track where Porsches of all types have traditionally done well, and continue to do so

all, been designed with just such an increase in mind. For this version, the bore was increased to 84mm, giving a capacity of 2,195 cc and an output of 230 hp at 7,800 revs. This was the version which ran between late 1969 and mid-1971, when the engine was further stretched to 2.4 litres. If 1970 had been a year of rallying successes equal to performances in GT races (European Rally Champions, 1st and 2nd at Monte Carlo and a trio of GT wins at Nürburgring, Spa and Monza), 1971 saw Porsche's attentions turning more to the GT events, where Le Mans and the Austrian GT victories were added to the previous year's clutch. In the Le Mans event, the 911 finished sixth overall.

The banning of Porsche's 917 from the World Championship of Makes in 1972 forced Porsche to consider developing the 911 to challenge in the 3-litre Class of the European GT Championships, in which it would face opposition from the likes of the more powerful Ferrari 365 and the de Tomaso Pantera. The homologation figure was set at 500 and the

RIGHT **The Porsche 911S. The 911S of Waldegaard and Helmer won the Monte Carlo rally in 1969, and again in 1970, other 911Ss coming in second and fourth places**

LEFT The Porsche 911 Carrera RSR Turbo form 1974. The previous year the RSR had notched up some famous wins on both sides of the Atlantic, and it repeated the act in 1974 with the European GT Championship going to John Fitzpatrick and the IMSA GT Championship to Peter Gregg

BELOW LEFT The 911 Carrera RSR Turbo seen here at Le Mans in Martini Racing team colours. The drivers were van Lennep and Muller

RIGHT **In 1976 Porsche
claimed a dual World
Championship; for
Production Sports Cars
and for Racing Sports
Cars. The photo shows
the victorious Martini
Racing Team with the
935 Turbo and the
winning Type 936 from
Le Mans. From left to
right, Manfred Schurti,
Rolf Stommelen, Race
Manager Manfred
Jantke, Jochem Mass
and Jacky Ickx**

technical requirements offered a stiff test. The new car would have to weigh in at 900 kg and the engine had to be opened up to over 2.5 litres to compete. It was a challenge which resulted in the Carerra RS and RSR, one of the finest examples found in the 911 family, which went on the market in 1972.

New cylinders were employed so that the bore could be opened to 90mm while retaining the same compression ratio, creating a capacity of 2.7 litres which delivered 210 hp at 6,300 revs. The car also sported wider wheels at the rear for the first time, and there was a rear spoiler to increase downforce. Fibreglass was used wherever possible to keep within the weight strictures. For the racing version, the Carrera RSR, the capacity was pushed up even further to 2,808 cc which generated over 300 hp at full throttle. It was an outstanding car. Mark Donohue, who drove a prototype in France, was so impressed that he immediately recommended that the cars be used for the 1974 International Race of Champions, to be held in California.

The RSR dominated the GT scene from 1973 to 1975, taking the European GT Championship overall, with the German Clemens Schickentanz finishing on level points with rival Frenchman Claude Ballot-Lena. Driven by the Muller-van Lepp pairing, it finished first overall in the Targa Florio, and there were firsts in the Nürburgring, Watkins Glen, Spa and Vallelunga GTs. The 911 RS made a brilliant start to its career In the US, it led a gruelling Daytona 24 hours to finish first overall for drivers Peter Gregg and Henry Haywood.

There was to be no resting on laurels either. The RS 2.8 was taken up to 3 litre capacity for the 1974 season, by using a number of ingenious modifications, resulting in a ten per cent increase in power.

Although they were not to be raced by the factory, the Carrera RSR 3.0s again swept all before them in the 1974 and 1975 seasons. They gained the 1974 FIA GT Cup with John Fitzpatrick at the wheel and recorded GT wins

LEFT **A Carrera in action at Brands Hatch during 1973. The Carreras were just ideal for the purpose; their successes on the track did a great deal of good for the sales of the road-going cars too**

BELOW LEFT **The Porsche Carrera RSR Turbo, in action during the 1974 season for the Martini Racing Team. The 2994cc engine of this version gave 315bhp, and tended to see off the competition with remarkable alacrity**

ABOVE **The 2000cc version of the Porsche 935, nicknamed the 'Baby', was built to take on the BMWs in the German Championship 2 litre class of 1977. Seen here in its Martini Porsche livery, the 'Baby' was fitted with a Turbocharged 1400cc engine**

RIGHT **The Porsche Turbo RSR of 1980 in road-going form**

at Monza, Spa, Imola, Nürburgring, Watkins Glen, Austria, Brands Hatch, Paul Ricard and Kyalami, with drivers such as Heyer, Loos, Gregg, Wolleck, Keller, Kremer and others cashing in on its ability. In the US, they won the IMSA championships against stiff opposition, particularly from the home-based Chevrolet Corvettes, powered by engines of almost twice the RSR's capacity. It was much the same story the following year: European Championship, IMSA Championship and a host of GT wins, including Le Mans. The icing on the cake was the first overall at Daytona for Gregg and Heywood. Something had to change and, as so often, it was the rules of

ABOVE LEFT **The Porsche 325 2 litre 'Baby' pictured in 1977, when Jacky Ickx won the Grand Prix supporting race in fine style. It was not, however the start of a long and illustrious career for the 'Baby'**

LEFT **The Martini Porsche 935 of 1976; Jacky Ickx and Jochen Mass won the World Championship for Makes event in the 935 the day after they had won the World Sportscar Championship. A good weekend by any standards!**

In 1977, Porsche won every round of the World Championship for Makes, four rounds going to the Martini Porsche team, the other five to customers. At the first race at the Nürburgring, the Loos 935, driven by an amalgamation of the drivers from the two Loos teams after the second car was forced to retire, was victorious, finishing ahead of the Kremer car of Wollek and Fitzpatrick

competition for GT races, and the RSR was effectively ruled offside. But Porsche had been ready for this and had a new model waiting in the wings, or rather three new models, the 934, the 935 and the 936.

These were all modified scions of the 930, the designation Porsche had given to the 911 Turbo, which they had begun work on in 1973. The 934 was for Group 4 (GT), 935 was a Manufacturer's World Championship contender, and the 936 was aimed at the Group 6 World Sportscar Championship. All three models won FIA Championships in their first season, 1976!

Porsche had already gained experience with turbocharging when developing the 917 that had been so successful in the Can-Am races. For the first model, a Carrera 2.14 litre engine was used, to meet the limits imposed on supercharged engines. This was something of a cobbled-together job (if such a phrase can ever be used about a Porsche engine!), borrowing components from a number of different units. The turbo used was by KKK and was fed from all six cylinders and the unit was housed at the extreme rear of the car. With turbo boost, power output was 490hp at 7,600 revs. The car was ready for the 1974 season and performed creditably, second at Le Mans to the mighty Mantras, which had so far seen off all challengers in the event since the Porsche 917 victory in 1971.

The 934 was developed as a racing car to fulfil the requirements of the new regulations established for the CSI Group 4 class, which meant that at least 400 models had to be built within two years. In general, cars eligible for this group could only have minor modifications from the standard model when racing. The 935 was designed for the Group 5 races, in which less stringent rules about modifications applied. The 936 was even more of an out-and-out racing car, a prototype in fact, with no pretensions to being a 'production' model in any way. And as already mentioned, all shared the 911 Turbo (930) as their design ancestor.

The 934's engine is perhaps best described as the 930 rethought. For the first time in the 911 range, it was single-ignition and used the K-Jetronic continuous flow injection system. Also for the first time in a Porsche, the intercooler was water-cooled, an option chosen to save space under the engine cover. The output for the 934 was given by the factory as 485hp at a low 7,000 rpm. Given that the specifications placed the car in the 4-litre to 4.5-litre class, in which the weight limit was a minimum of 1,120kg, Porsche had a lot of room for leeway, and in many cases a lead ballast was used in the nose to modify the car's centre of gravity. There was even weight to spare to allow for electric windows!

Their racing career followed the pattern set by the RSRs – they were virtually unbeatable, the only significant setback coming at the 1976 Le Mans event, in which an army of different Porsche teams were present, when, perhaps to the embarrassment of the factory, a Carrera RSR 3.0 took the GT first place. Things sometimes fall out that way, and, besides, the overall winner was the specially-prepared 936, driven by the formidable team of Jacky Ickx and Gijs van Lennep. Fans of the 934 could also take ample consolation from Porsche's fourth consecutive European GT Championship gained by Dutchman Toine Hezemans and the Trans-Am Championship across the Atlantic, with George Follmer at the wheel. However, interest in the GT class was beginning to decline, and Porsche put no further development work into the car, although it carried on competing successfully in a number of events worldwide for a number of years to come.

For the 935, the engine was modified to have a power output of around 590hp at full boost. In the first year only two cars were produced for the World Championship of Makes races. Initially, Porsche met with difficulties when the authorities ruled that the distinctive rear spoiler, housing the bulky intercooler, was illegal and last minute changes had to be made. The model finally came good at Watkins Glen and Dijon, but the competition went to the final race of the season before the title was safely in Porsche's hands. It was in 1977 that the 935 fully came into its own, after further development work at the factory. From then on it was to be Porsche's flagship car for three seasons, gaining victories in the Trans-Am, the IMSA Championship, Daytona and just about every other track on the circuit. A number of

vehicles were produced for private customers – a total of around thirty cars in all.

The 936 was a prototype developed with Le Mans in mind, and stretched the basic design of the engine to its limits. It brought victory to the Ickx-van Lennep partnership in 1976 and its return, in heavily modified form, was eagerly anticipated in 1977. It was this race which confirmed Ickx as a superstar in sports car racing, if any confirmation was needed. Following piston failure in his car, Ickx switched to Porsche's second car in the race, which itself had already been in the pits with pump failure. Ickx was in 41st place and half an hour off the lead, but drove like a man inspired throughout the night, constantly exceeding previous lap records to reach second place by morning. The 936 won, but its piston had cracked too – the engine simply couldn't deal with the stresses being placed upon it.

LEFT **The Jagermeister 935 from 1977, one of a clutch of 935s that helped Porsche win the Championship of Makes, thanks to the efforts of their works and their customer teams**

BELOW **The Porsche 935 in long-tail form for 1978, which became known as 'Moby Dick', supposedly because it reminded someone of a whale, which seems less than complimentary to a car that started its career by setting a new lap record at Silverstone, and winning the race by a clear seven laps**

A heavily modified 935 was used for 1978, the 935/78 'Moby Dick', probably the fastest version of the 911 ever built, recording a straight speed in Le Mans practice of 227.5 mph (see chapter 6). Thereafter, the factory increasingly left it to private teams to carry the company's flag, most notably the Kremer brothers, Porsche devotees who specialized in preparing production-derived models to racing standard. Both these are discussed in greater detail in the following chapter.

One further development of the 911 deserves special mention – the four-wheel drive 959 and its racing version, the 961. The initial production target of the 959 was to be 200 and these were snapped up as soon as

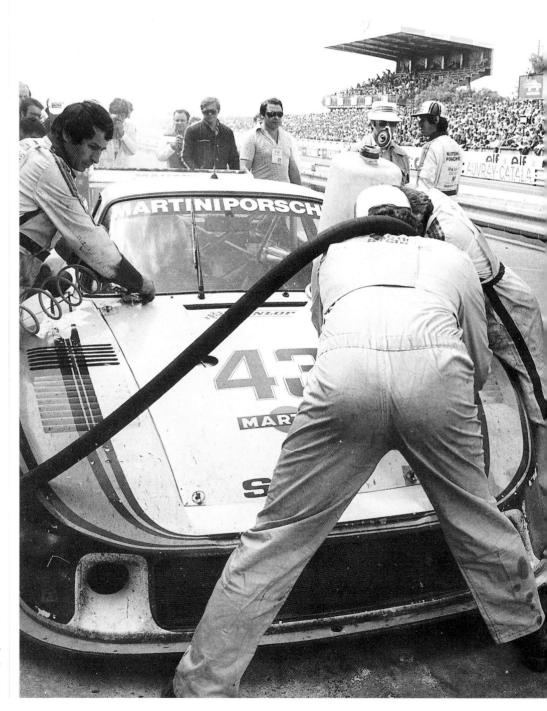

RIGHT **The long-tailed 935 'Moby Dick', designated 935/78, is refuelled at Le Mans in 1978. The Group 5 car was being driven by Schurti and Stommelen on this occasion**

the project was announced. The car was soon worth nearly three times its production price – and that wasn't exactly cheap – such was the demand. The bodywork was radically reformed to produce exeptionally low drag with zero lift. Lightweight materials were used wherever possible, so that apart from a crash resistant passenger shell, lightweight rein-

forced resins, aluminium and fibreglass were employed. The engine was a modified version of the early 935, changed for road use to reduce noise and make maintenance easier. It employed two turbochargers in a complex arrangement which reduced the exhaust back pressure and so increased efficiency at higher speeds. The output was 450hp at 6,500 rpm, devastating in a road-legal car and translating into the following performance figures: 0 – 60mph in 3.6 secs, 0 – 100mph in 8.3 secs and a top speed of 197 mph. No wonder people were queuing up to get their hands on one – even at the stated factory price of (cont. p 100)

LEFT **The 6 cylinder 911 engine developing 620bhp, as fitted to the 962C; strictly not for amateurs**

BELOW LEFT **Cutaway of the magnificent 959, surely one of the most covetable 911 derivative 'production' cars; or rather, one of the most covetable road cars ever, full stop. Impressive as the racing 961: staggering on the autobahn**

RALLYING PORSCHE

The mainstay of Porsche's competitions activities has been endurance racing, but there have been some notable successes in other areas: Porsche has a single Grand Prix victory to its credit, Dan Gurney's French GP victory in 1962, many more as the maker of the TAG-McLaren Formula One engine, an Indycar victory (Teo Fabi at Mid-Ohio in 1989), and some great rally victories to the credit of the 911 family.

The Porsche 911's competitions debut was on the Monte Carlo Rally in 1965, when engineers Herbert Linge and Peter Falk unexpectedly won the GT category, and three years later the factory prepared a Monte 'works' team for Vic Elford and Pauli Toivonen. Elford and his co-driver David Stone won the event outright in their 911T with Toivonen second, and the Finn went on to win the World Rally Championship for Porsche. Bjorn Waldegard won the Swedish Rally in February

1968, and then won the Monte Carlo Rally twice in succession in 1969 and in 1970. Although there was a lull in activities after that (Porsche ran the six-cylinder 914 model in 1974 without success), the 911 came back for one more surprise victory in 1978, when Jean-Pierre Nicolas won an unusual Monte Carlo Rally.

In fact Nicolas arrived in the principality as the winner just as Prince Rainier was preparing to present the Car of the Year Award to Professor Fuhrmann, for the design of the 928,

so it was a double celebration for Porsche. The Porsche 959 was conceived as a Group B race competitor but the regulations evolved away from it and towards the small, light-weight machines such as the Peugeot 205 Rallye. Instead, and at the urging of Jack Ickx, the four-wheel drive car was developed for the punishing Paris-Dakar Raid rally, with some outstanding success. Ickx himself was not lucky, hampered by a burned wiring loom in 1984, but Frenchman René Metge drove his 911 4wd car to an impressive victory. Entries were not successful in 1985 but Metge won the desert raid again in 1986, this time with the definitive 959 model with its sophisticated 4wd system providing an invaluable aid.

around £140,000, Porsche could scarcely have covered their production costs. This was state of the art racing technology, not a fashion statement. The first cars were delivered to customers in 1987, two years later than originally promised, but it was worth the wait for the fortunate two hundred.

Porsche had used this time to test every aspect of the package. They entered perhaps the most gruelling race of all, the Paris-Dakar Rally, under Rothmans sponsorship and with Jacky Ickx leading the driving team. The first attempt was in 1984, although the model was little more than a 911 Carrera 3.2 modified for four-wheel drive. It duly won with René Metge and the other two entrants completed the 8,000 mile course, finishing 6th and 26th overall. By 1986, the car was virtually a finished production version and Metge and Ickx finished 1st and 2nd respectively, while the third entry, packed with back-up spares came home 5th, driven by Dipl Ing Roland Kussmaul, who had overseen the development of the project. The final test came at Le Mans in the same year, where, as the 961 and trimmed

down to racing mode, it came a creditable seventh and was timed at 204 mph in the straight.

The latter part of the 1980s also saw the development of the 911 Turbo on more conventional lines. The first of these models was the 911 SC/RS designed for both GT races and rallying. This development was continued with a number of models in a similar vein. In 1992 the 964-based Carrera RS was launched, with a capacity of 3.6 litres, a road-going version of the cars the company had produced for the Carrera Cup races it had inaugurated in 1990 as successor to the Porsche Cup. In a similar mould was the 911 Turbo S, a production verion of the 911 Turbo which had won the 1991 IMSA Supercar Championship. This was another Porsche thoroughbred, capable of 0-100 mph in 9.2 seconds and with a top speed of 180 mph, a car which felt at home ticking over in traffic, but suddenly taking on a whole new persona when the turbo kicked in at 3,500 revs.

The 3.6 might seem to have been the end of the line for the development of an engine that started out at 2 litres, but yet another redesign

of the block resulted in the Carrera RSR 3.8 litre which came first in the Spa 24-hour race in 1993 and first in GT class at Le Mans in the same year. One hundred models were built for enthusiasts, and it was a privately-owned vehicle, almost straight from the factory, that gained the Le Mans GT victory.

Due partly to its greater accessibility, interest in GT racing which had been in decline for a number of years, began to increase in the mid-1990s, and Porsche saw it as a natural arena in which to demonstrate their prowess. The RSR 3.8 was an ideal foundation for development into the new millennium. A specially prepared one-off, the 911 Le Mans Turbo indicated the company's renewed commitment to its tradition of competition. It won its first outing at Sebring 1993, but retired from the Le Mans race following a minor accident.

The RSR 3.8 line has been extended with the turbocharged 911 GT2 and GT2 Evolution which campaigned around the world in private hands during the 1995 and 1996 seasons. The GT2 developed 450hp, while the GT Evo offers a thumping 600bhp.

For the 1996 Le Mans, Porsche were keen to take the outright honours from McLaren who had won the 1995 race, and from Ferrari who had a strong contender in the F40. It was an ambitious policy, since the public interest was such that any failure would be wide open to scrutiny. The car, designated GT1, was based on the GT2 Evolution, although the modifications were extensive.

The dramas of the race didn't help. Nevertheless, they took 2nd and 3rd places overall, first and second in the GT class, and left the racing world in no doubt that Porsche was back in the game. Lap times taken at Le Mans, Brands Hatch and Spa demonstrated that it was by a long way the quickest car racing that season. 1997 was the same kind of story – but maybe more agonising for the team. A lap in hand and two hours 15 minutes from the flag and Ralf Kellener's bid for victory came to a fiery end, becoming one of the 31 cars from 48, dnf. More on this in chapter 5. The new road 911 for 1998 will have its first dohc powerplant and 4 valves per cylinder, plus far better drag: going racing? Of course.

ABOVE Hans-Joachim Stuck in a 911 Turbo won seven of the nine races in the 1993 IMSA Championship for the Brumos team and for Porsche. This was his first American title in his 24-year racing career, and during the season he notched up record times in practice over and over again – as well as winning most of the races of course

CHAPTER FIVE

THE LURE OF LE MANS

PREVIOUS PAGE
The fabulous GT1
(fabulous enough
anyway, to make
McLaren lodge
complaints regarding GT
eligibility!) blasts down
the straight at Le Mans
in 1996

RIGHT For Le Mans in
1980, Porsche decided
against running the 936s,
which had not performed
really well there for two
years, and went instead
for three 924 Carreras.
By half-way through the
race, the 924s were in
eighth, ninth and tenth
places, but in the event
only the car driven by
Barth finished, in a
respectable but not
outstanding sixth place

BELOW RIGHT By
winning the Le Mans 24-
hour race in 1985, Klaus
Ludwig, Paolo Barilla
and John Winter, driving
a Joest New Man
Porsche 956, gave
Porsche its tenth
outright victory there
since 1970 – a record
number of wins for a
single car marque in one
of the world's most
famous races

The gladiatorial arena of the Circuit Permanent de la Sarthe, Le Mans, holds an enduring fascination for followers of motorsport. Only Daytona on the other side of the Atlantic approaches it in the intensity of the racing, but the atmosphere at Le Mans is something else again. For the week of the '24 Heures', the town turns into a festival of the fastest cars in the world, and it is not only the endurance of the cars that is tested to the limit. Many of the 200,000 plus followers are ready for a long rest after the racing is over, having endured either extremes of midsummer sun or one of Le Mans' infamous downpours. (One of the editor's favourite comments on the event is from David Phipps in the 1966 *Autocourse* annual: 'Everything about Le Mans is on a vast scale. The circuit is 8.36 miles long, the car parks are anything up to two miles away – and you can pay up to 3/6d for a bottle of lemonade.' Plus ça change.)

Since its first outing in 1951, Porsche has arrived at the Sarthe circuit each year to take

on the other manufacturers. In fact, either as a factory team or in the hands of private teams, there has not been a year since then that there has not been a Porsche, a record matched by no other make. The Porsche presence really began to turn into a flood with the development of the 904 in 1964. From then on Porsche was the dominant manufacturer at the event, often turning up mob-handed with customers making up half the total entry.

In fact, since 1951, around 25 per cent of the cars that have been entered for Le Mans have been Porsches, and one in every three cars that have made it to the finish of the marathon have been from Porsche Stuttgart. The figures are even more astonishing when one remembers that it was not until 1970 that Porsche gained its first victory at the track. Despite what fans of rival makes might secretly wish, Le Mans without Porsche is simply unthinkable.

The full story of Porsche's many assaults on the Le Mans trophy and its battles with rivals such as Ford, Lola, Mirage, Renault, Ferrari and McClaren would be the subject of another dozen books. The previous chapters have looked at the development of the major Porsche racing models. But things would be incomplete without an account of some of the great moments of Porsche triumph at the track and at some of the cars and drivers to thrill the crowds over the years.

The real glory years began in the 1970s, but it is worth looking back just before, to 1969 and a defeat. The white army was led by a brace of the awesome 917s, with four 908s bringing up the rear. The 917's strategy was simple, as strategies usually are at Le Mans – to grind the opposition into the ground by building up an unassailable lead. But the 917s were still too new to have developed the reliability that Le Mans requires and were forced to retire. With

RIGHT The Porsche cars wait in the pits before the start of the Le Mans race in 1968. Porsche's contingent of four 908s and three 907s only managed a second and third place between them in the race, which was, unusually, held in September rather than June that year

BELOW RIGHT The L'Arbre Racing Team 911 GT2 at Le Mans in 1996. Private Racing teams have always been a very important part of the Porsche racing mix, at Le Mans and elsewhere. Engine designation Type M 64/60, the same air-cooled Boxer, with the two exhaust turbochargers

four hours to go there were only two cars left with any realistic chance of victory – the Ford GT40 with Jacky Ickx at the wheel and a Porsche 908, driven by Hans Herrmann (their partners were Jack Oliver and Gerard Larrousse respectively). The final duel was immense, the two cars passing and repassing each other as the time ebbed away. At the finish, Ickx was ahead with Herrmann an agonising 70 metres behind. Never had the line between victory and defeat been drawn so fine.

The drama was continued in the following year, with Herrmann having one last crack at the race, this time in a Porsche 917, sharing with Richard Attwood. The teething troubles of the 917 had by now ben ironed out and confidence was high, Ferrari appearing to be the chief rival. The clouds opened. Ferrari crashed out in a pile-

up at Maison Blanche and it was a question of which of the two 917s remaining would hold out. There was no doubt on whose side the spectators' hopes were pinned. The dream result came true – the 917 driven by the Siffert/Redman team blew and it was Herrmann who took victory and consolation for the previous year's disappointment, announcing his retirement shortly after receiving the winner's trophy.

That man Jacky Ickx is as important to Le Mans as is Porsche. He was to deny Porsche first place again in 1975, when they entered

LEFT **The calm before the storm; cars line up for inspection prior to the start, a moment of tension that is difficult to communicate if you haven't been there. A bottle of champagne to the first reader to write to the publishers identifying the year; there are plenty of clues. Incidentally, the designer of this book, who has fortuitously avoided arrest at the Automobile Club de L'Ouest 'Welcome Bar' for the last three races, is not allowed to enter**

FAR RIGHT The shadows lengthen as Saturday evening comes to Le Mans during the 1996 race – the major part of the race still left to run, and everything to drive for

ABOVE RIGHT The Porsche 911 GT2 of L'Arbre Racing team from France, during the Le Mans race of 1996. Drivers were Patrice Goueslard, Andre Ahrle and Partick Bourdais.

CENTRE RIGHT The Porsche 911 GT2 of Elf Haberthur Racing team from Switzerland, during the Le Mans Race of 1996. The drivers were Michel Neugarten, Toni Seiler and Bruno Ilien

BELOW RIGHT And another Porsche 911 GT2, this time from New Hardware/Parr Motorsport, a New-Zealand team based in the UK. The drivers: Bill Farmer, Greg Murphy and Robert Nearn. The GT2 Evolution is of course designed to meet Le Mans GT1 regulations. It weighs 1150kg, and for comparison, that's 100kg more than the GT1, 350kg less than a road 911 Turbo. The GT2 produces 450 BHP, the GT2 Evolution is up there with the GT1, with 600 BHP

two of their virtually untried turbocharged Carrera RSRs. One of the pair exceeded expectations by finishing second, to Ickx in the 3-litre Gulf-Mirage GR8. Well, if you can't beat them, hire them – Ickx was driving for Porsche the following season and took the first of four overall victories for the company – 1976, 1977, 1981 and 1982. The last two victories came in partnership with Derek Bell, surely the leading candidates for the title of the most formidable pairing ever to compete at Le Mans.

It was of course during the 1980s that Porsche made Le Mans almost an outpost of Stuttgart, as victory followed victory in a record-breaking undefeated run from 1981 to 1988, when Jaguar finally wrested the trophy away. Although the run was begun by the Ickx/Bell 936, it was the astonishing 956s and

ABOVE **The Parsche 906, also known as the Carrera 6, was designed by Ferdinand Piech, and based on a modified form of the 911 engine. It had an extremely light frame, and a highly aerodynamic bodyline**

their 962 derivatives which ruled the roost. The 1983 race saw an entry of no fewer than eleven 956s from various teams. It was a procession, the Rothmans-sponsored factory cars making circuit after circuit on rails, coming home one-two-three. This time Ickx and Bell were edged out by team-mates Schuppan, Holbert and Haywood, but that was academic. The minor places were made up by Porsche 935s, with a Ferrari sixth and yet another Porsche in seventh. Of the eleven Porsche starters, only two failed to complete – no wonder the other teams despaired.

The following year there were no factory entries – the politics of motorsport had caused

Porsche to withdraw in protest. Nevertheless, there were twelve 956s at the start, all run by private teams. Again the race resembled a high roller Porsche Cup. It was thrilling stuff and could have gone to any of four teams up until the last hour – all of them Porsches. As it was, Porsche cars claimed all top seven places, with Klaus Ludwig and Henri Pescarolo gaining victory for the deservedly popular Joest team.

The Joest team repeated the performance in 1985; the works team, which had come back into the fray, suffering unexpected engine failure. But it was also the year when the drivers were beginning to realise just what a thin

line they were treading at Le Mans. Jacky Ickx retired from racing after Stefan Bellof suffered a fatal crash when trying to overtake him. The cars were simply becoming too fast for the track, which consisted in the main, after all, of ordinary roads which were in public use for the rest of the year. Grit, determination and courage married with skill is one thing; pushing your luck, quite another.

Derek Bell, Hans Stuck and Al Holbert became the Porsche works strike team for the 1986 season, and strike they did, again making it seem easy as they took first place, in front of six other Porsches. But yet again, Le Mans had taken its toll, with the Austrian Jo

LEFT **Closely contested corner during the 1996 Le Mans race. Porsches, as (almost) always, everywhere you look**

BELOW LEFT **The Roock Racing Team Porsche 911 GT2 Evolution at Le Mans in 1996. The German team's drivers: Jean-Pierre Jarier, Jesus Pareja and Dominic Chappell**

RIGHT The Le-Mans
class-winning works
team Porsche GT1
notches up another
victory. The twin exhaust
turbos are KKK K27.2
with 35.7mm restrictors.
Bosch ABS is permitted
only for Le Mans

Gartner fatally losing control of his Kremer Porsche in the early hours of the morning. The next year was a closer-run thing, with only the works Porsche left in the race after a few hours. Jaguar, the major competition, suffered bad luck throughout, but had seen enough to realize that Porsche were now vulnerable. The Bell/Stuck/Holbert team had had to fight hard for their victory this time and, in a sense, it was a fitting end to an extraordinary era of racing. In 1988 Jaguar were back and hungry. If anything this was a more energy-sapping, nerve-jangling race than the previous year's. The cars were developed to such an extent that the fine edge between success and catastrophic failure could hardly be gauged. Stuck set the fastest lap in the Porsche 962C at a fraction under 150 mph, but the Jaguar XJR under the guidance of Jan Lammers and team-mates Johnny Dumfries and Andy Wallace coaxed their car home, two and a half minutes ahead of the works Porsche. Honour was satisfied and the two heavyweights could pay their respects to each other as equals.

LEFT **The Courage Porsche team on 'home ground' in 1996; the Le Mans based team's car was driven by Mario Andretti, Jan Lammers and Derek Warwick**

BELOW **The victorious GT1; Porsche's two GT1s, numbered 25 and 26 swept aside all competition to take the class honours in fine style – though not overall victory. Drivers of 25 were Hans-Joachim Stuck, Thierry Boutsen and Bob Wollek. Two auxiliary Litronic headlamps are fitted for Le Mans**

TOP RIGHT **One of the two Courage Porsche cars that took on Le Mans in 1996**

ABOVE RIGHT **The Kremer Porsche Spyder K8 – carrying number one – during the 1996 Le Mans race. Drivers were Christophe Bouchut, Harri Toivonen and Jurgen Laessig**

CENTRE RIGHT **The Joest Racing team's second 1996 Le Mans entrant, based on the 962. Drivers were 1997 winner Michele Alboreto, Pierluigi Martini and Didier Theys**

BELOW RIGHT **The other half of the famous Le Mans '96 duo 'number 25 & number 26' Porsche's drivers were Yannick Dalmas, Karl Wendlinger and Scott Goodyear**

RIGHT The support team's role is vital to the success of any enterprise; never more so than during the progress of a race. When the leading GT1 blew up in the last few hours of Le Mans 1997, one mechanic was seen to burst into tears of disbelief

Porsche's interest in Group C racing was waning in 1988, as Formula 1 looked more rewarding and prestigious and Indycar more attractive in marketing terms in the States. Indeed, Porsche's temporary winding-down of interest was soon followed by the FIA's decision to alter the Group C regulations in favour of 3.5 litre racing engines, when Jaguar, Mercedes, Peugeot and Toyota became the major players.

Following an exceedingly poor Le Mans race in 1992, when only 22 Group C cars could be assembled for the 24-hours, the ACO took matters back in their own hands and made GT cars the backbone of the race in 1993.

Porsche ran a special version of the Turbo model for Hans Stuck. Hurley Haywood and Walter Rohrl, but the unfortunate Rohrl ran into the back of a slower competitor during Saturday evening and damaged the oil cooler, putting the car out of the race.

Porsche had a bold plan for 1994, though, taking Jochen Dauer's street conversion of the 962 model as the base for a Grand Tourer! Dauer, a real enthusiast and racer who makes his money from leather goods, was delighted to become the figurehead for the works team at Le Mans, with unlimited assistance to get the road car conversion fully homologated within European Community regulations.

Two of these cars, Dauer 962 LM Porsche GTs to give them their full title, were entered for the 24-hour race, in fact with Reinhold Joest's racing crew helping in the pits. Hans Stuck, Danny Sullivan and Thierry Boutsen claimed pole position for the race, even ahead of the SARD and Trust team Group C Toyotas with Yannick Dalmas, Hurley Haywood and Mauro Baldi qualifying fifth.

The contest between Group C and GT was even and exciting, the sports cars with smaller fuel tanks which meant they had to stop more

often, and the race reached a climax when Eddie Irvine's SARD Toyota pulled over with a broken gear linkage less than two hours from the finish. Dalmas, Haywood and Baldi offered up a prayer as they sped to the chequered flag, leaving Irvine to fend off Stick's car by a narrow margin.

The audacious move to legalise a racing car was too much for the ACO, who tightened up their homologation requirements for 1995. Porsche went onto the back foot with the GT2 model, a genuine 911 based car with twin tur-bochargers, wing and spoiler, and around 500 horsepower for the drivers.

Porsche were outclassed throughout 1995 by the $1million McLaren F1 GTR which won

Le Mans at its first attempt, although Mario Andretti and Bob Wollek managed second place on their Porsche powered Courage C36, delayed by an accident on Saturday evening.

It was time for Porsche to rethink. Their TWR sports car based IMSA contender was heavily handicapped just before Daytona, leading to the withdrawal of the works team, and Porsche chairman Dr Wendelin Wiedeking bravely gave the go-ahead for an entirely new GT model. It was based only loosely on the 911, with the 3.2 litre twin-turbo engine mounted ahead of the rear wheels.

The Porsche GT1 was a sensational car when it made its debut at Le Mans, first at the qualifying weekend in April, then in the 24-hour

LEFT **The team in action; teamwork has always been one of the mainstays of the Weissach philosophy; teamwork between Porsche and their race-going customers, teamwork among research, design and testing departments within the Porsche organisation, and teamwork among drivers, mechanics, engineers and race managers, before, during and after the races**

RIGHT **Final detailed checks for the GT1. 27/65-18 tyres front, 30/70-18 rear**

FAR RIGHT **The Porsche GT1 undergoes a tyre change and a clean, as well as taking on a change of driver during the 1996 Le Mans race. Additional body panels were actually flown in from Weissach after the practice sessions**

race in June. Powered by a fully water-cooled engine, a variation on the Boxster power unit, the GT1 vied for pole position with – of all things – the TWR Porsche WSC cars which the factory loaned to Reinhold Joest.

Porsche's management was certain that the GT1 cars, with 600 horsepower and equipped with 100 litre fuel tanks, would beat the 550 horsepower 'prototypes' with 80 litre fuel tanks, but loaned the two WSC cars to Joest as a precaution, a back-up in case the GT1s failed in their task.

The two GT1s, prepared at Weissach and run by factory personnel, were driven by well trusted drivers, Hans Stuck, Bob Wollek and Thierry Boutsen in one car, the other piloted by Yannick Dalmas, Scott Goodyear and Karl Wendlinger.

The two Porsche GT1s were completely reliable, more so than perhaps their drivers. In the course of the 24-hour race all six drivers were reported to have spun, and the stock of replacement undertrays was exhausted by Sunday morning. "If our drivers go off the road once more, we cannot repair their cars effectively" said competitions director Herbert Ampferer.

Porsche's joy was in fact to be confined as the Joest Racing TWR Porsche WSC entry won the race in the hands of Manuel Reuter, Davy Jones and Alexander Wurz, a single lap ahead

of Stuck, Wollek and Boutsen, with the other Porsche GT1 of Dalmas, Wendlinger and Goodyear further back in third position. The 'works' cars were first and second in the Grand Touring category, with the McLarens fourth, fifth and sixth overall; but the race had not gone at all as planned: worse to come in '97, with a works McLaren BMW F1 GTR in the field for the first time …

Later in '96, the Porsche GT1s were driven to easy victories in the BPR Global Endurance GT Cup series races at Brands Hatch, Spa-Francorchamps and the new Chinese track at Zhuhai. The last victory of the season went to Emmanuel Collard and Ralf Kelleners, then current and previous Porsche Supercup winners who were justly rewarded with a 'works' car in China, and drove a faultless race.

RIGHT **Night-time at Le Mans; everything changes at night. Spectators drift off into the dark for a few hours sleep, or to eat, drink and be loud in the village. Other spectators arrive, with blankets and flasks, for a few hours watching – sometimes with a whole stand section populated by half a dozen people. But in the garages and pit lane, the action is the same as in daylight hours, with no let up in sight until Sunday afternoon**

BELOW RIGHT **The cars come and go; a few minutes of frantic activity in the pit lane, but more time spent behind the scenes analysing data, interpreting signs, processing feed back from drivers, working out how to gain the precious few minutes that will make the difference. Though all the data in the world will not help you if your car is practically obliterated, as was the Kremer car in a crash in 1997. Or if a tiny solder on your oil cooler melts and brings you to a dead stop, as happened to Martin Brundle in the superfast Nissan R390 that year**

The Porsche GT2 was extremely success-ful in the GT2 category in 1995 and 1996, a regular winner for teams such as Stadler Motorsport (Enzo Calderari and Lilian Bryner) Franz Konrad (often with Bob Wollek co-dri-ving) and Roock Racing whose Porsche was dominant in 1996 in the hands of Ralf Kelleners, Bruno Eichmann and Gerd Ruch.

Roock Racing's victory in the GT2 division at Le Mans was especially praiseworthy as Kelleners, Eichman and Guy Martinolle had a near faultless run to 12th place overall. The Chevrolet powered Marcos was a strong com-petitor, sometimes quicker in qualifying and three times a winner in 1996, but Cor Euser's Marcos team was outgunned by a score of Porsche GT2s which competed regularly in the BPR Global Endurance GT Cup series.

The Porsche Le Mans story would not be complete without some mention of the Kremer brothers who have become something of a Porsche institution. Edwin Kremer has been a successful Porsche driver since the introduc-tion of the 911, winning the Porsche Cup in 1971. His brother Manfred is technical director of the Cologne-based operation specializing in producing Porches to race specification. Their efforts were to come to fruition in 1979, when they entered their 935 K3 for the race. According to the Kremers, there were over 100 modifications made to their standard produc-tion model, including better streamlining, a stiffer structure and the use of an air/air cooler rather than employing water-cooling. The resulting improvement in performance they estimated at a conservative one per cent – but at this level one per cent goes a long way. The figures for the car read: 0 to 60 mph in 3.0 secs and 0 to 100 mph in 5.8 secs from an engine developing 750 bhp. The race was one littered with breakdowns and it came down to a battle for survival. The rain didn't help either. The Kremer car lost nearly an hour when the injec-tion pump failed, but they had established enough of a lead to hold on to first place against challengers who also suffered prob-lems. It may not have been a classic race, but it was a popular victory and repayment for the Kremer brother's commitment to the marque and to the Sarthe event. Although regular visi-tors, they would have to wait until 1987 to achieve their next best result, a fourth place.

Two specific cars also deserve to be mentioned as part of the Le Mans legend. The first is the unforgettable Pink Pig, alias Big Bertha, the Trüffeljäger von Zuffenhausen. Under its skin it was just a 917: but what a skin! When it was first seen during the test days of the 1971 event, the white car was considered to be one of the ugliest looking pieces of machinery ever to grace the Sarthe circuit. Designed by the Paris-based studio SERA, its pronounced side overhang, designed to keep the wheels out of the airstream but not locked inconveniently away under spats, meant a porcine 7 ft 4 in

width. The idea was to try to combine the major virtue of the long-tail Le Mans cars – low drag – with the handling of the short-tailed sprint versions of the 917. Aware that their latest creation was raising a few eyebrows, Porsche painted it pink and divided up that fat body into butcher's cuts of meat, from 'rüssel' (snout) to 'schwanz' (tail). Drivers Reinhold Joest and Willi Kauhsen showed that the design had great potential in the race, before running off the road because of faulty newly fitted discs. Big Bertha would never race again, as the 917 era drew to a close.

LEFT **The Kremer K4, a modified version of the Porsche 935 produced by Kremer when they got wind of the imminent arrival of the Porsche works team's lastest offering, the long-tailed 'Moby Dick', in 1978. The 935's bodywork is modified to increase the rake of the windscreen**

BELOW LEFT **The car that caused the consternation at Kremer; 'Moby Dick' otherwise known as the Porsche 935/78 long-tail**

The classic Porsche racers such as this 935/78 'Moby Dick', and the short-tail 'Baby' 935, can be seen in the Porsche museum at Zuffenhausen, along with many examples of classic Porsche road-cars and one offs from Porsche's incredible history. But while celebrating the works cars and sports prototypes, we should not forget the little guys: in the same year (1983) that nine out the first ten finishers were Porsches, back in 22nd place was chassis 840225, a near standard 928 ...

The second car is notable as the perfect example of Porsche's ability to push the regulations in force at any one time to the limit. Moby Dick, the great white whale, was type 935/78, built according to the 'silhouette' formula, which allowed for modifications but was meant to ensure that the racing version retained a basic similarity to the road going model from which it was derived. But all that was left of the 911 in the look of Moby Dick after Porsche had done their streamlining tricks was part of the roof line, the hood and the windscreen! What were supposed to be wheel arch extensions at the front were in fact completely new fenders plus a transverse air dam. The end plates on the swooping tail were enormous. Viewed from the side, you might think that there is a chunk of bodywork missing – and you would be more or less right. Porsche had intended to join the front and rear fenders and cover the doors completely, but FISA put their foot down and demanded that the fairing stop about a third of the way along. As for the innards, the modifications were extensive enough according to Porsche for the 3.2-litre engine to generate about 750 bhp with the use of water cooled cylinder heads, also fitted to the 936. There was enough cooling now for a four-valve cylinder head layout, with a consequent rise in engine speed and power. The 935/78 won its debut race, the Silverstone 1,000 kms in the hands of Ickx and Mass, but suffered an incurable misfire at Le Mans and finished a disappointing eighth.

So what happened in 1997? Well, confidence was high that the works GT1s would take overall victory and with two hours to go it looked as if Ralf Kelleners, (Yannick Dalmas and Emmanuel Collard his co-drivers) had done it. Suddenly, flames shot from the engine and within seconds the car was a charred shell. It would be a Porsche prototype which would take the honours again, the Joest TWR Porsche that had been stalking the GT1 lap after lap, waiting for failure. The Gulf and Schnitzer McLarens couldn't close the gap on ex F1 driver Michele Alboreto. Co-driver Kristensen provided fastest lap: 135.20 mph.

TOP LEFT **The GT1 that could be looked at, admired and, provided you were a responsible and careful-looking adult, touched, outside the Porsche garage at Le Mans. There have been many milestones for Porsche at Sarthe. 1958 for example, and the first Porsche to average more than 100 mph – 101.22 mph for the Behra/Herrmann RSK Spyder. Or 1971 and the magnesium chassis 917K of Helmut Marko and Gijs Van Lennep set the awesome record of 138.13 mph. The GT1 is another Le Mans milestone for Porsche**

LEFT **The Porsche Factory Team 1996 take a bow. Porsche in their magazine 'Christophorus' congratulate the team: 'They turned night into day, and ignored both Sundays and holidays in recent months; a total of 94 employees at Porsche Motorsport realised the two 911 GT1 cars from the first pencil line to runs on a track in just 243 days.' The fruits of their labour of course began with GT success at Le Mans**

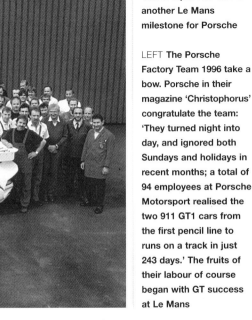

CHAPTER SIX

GRAND PRIX AND INDY

The latter half of the fifties had seen a tightening up of FIA Formula One regulations; the alcohol-based 'home brew' fuels were banned in 1958, with a standard 100-130 octane commercial petrol introduced as standard. The changes for 1961 were substantial; maximum engine capacity was reduced from 2500 cc to 1500 cc, a minimum weight limit of 450 kg was introduced, roll-bars, on-board starters, battery cut-outs and double braking systems became obligatory, enclosed wheels were banned, as was the taking on of oil during the course of a race. As well as improving safety, the changes were designed to brighten up the Formula races somewhat by attracting new competitors, and the Porsche experts soon realised that here was a type of car with which they were already familiar – in theory at least.

The first Porsche Formula One cars, built for the 1961 season, were based on the successful Formula Two 718 racers, and designated 787. Porsche began development of a dedicated power unit for it, but fitted it with the tried and tested 4-cylinder 547/3 engine in the meantime. The services of two proven drivers, Dan Gurney and Joakim Bonnier were secured, and Porsche's Formula 1 assault was

PREVIOUS PAGES **The 1962 F1 804, fitted with a new 8-cylinder engine. Hopes were high, but Porsche would disappear from the F1 scene at the end of the season – for the next twenty years**

RIGHT **The TAG Marlboro McLaren with its innovative V6 Porsche-designed power unit was very successful in the 1984 season, with Niki Lauda and Alain Prost winning between them twelve of the sixteen races**

ready to roll. But all did not go according to plan. The first race was at Brussels, then came Monaco and Zandvoort. Neither driver was happy with the handling or the speed of the 787, and a quick switch back to 718/2s was made for the remainder of the season. Porsche did not win a Grand Prix that year, although Gurney managed to come equal third in the driver's championship by virtue of sheer determination, and only narrowly missed winning at Rheims.

Understandably, everyone, including Porsche's racing manager Huschke von Hanstein, had high hopes for the 1962 season: the new 8-cylinder engine, designated 753, was ready, and Porsche had designed an improved car for it – the 804. There should have been a big improvement in fortunes, but the first race at Zandvoort showed the new car to be underpowered and problematic. Monte Carlo was a disaster. Porsche decided to pass on the round at Spa in favour of some serious readjustments back at base. They returned at Rouen, and to everyone's delight, Gurney finished in first place. He triumphed again at Solitude, with Bonnier taking second place, although unfortunately for everyone the race did not count towards the Championship. There were great expectations for the remainder of the season, especially the Nürburgring, but there were no further victories and some disappointing technical hitches. At the end of the season, Porsche decided to quit Formula One completely.

It was to be twenty years before Porsche ventured again into the world of Formula One racing, and this time it would be as an engine manufacturer not a constructor. Porsche were asked by Techniques d'Avant Garde (TAG) to design a new engine for McLaren. The innovative V6 power unit that they produced was immediately successful in its first season in 1984. Niki Lauda and Alain Prost won between

LEFT **The Porsche 787 Formula 1 contender of 1961 was based on the successful Formula 2 718 racers. At the Zuffenhausen works, the car is inspected by racing engineer Wilhelm Hild** *(left)* **and Ferdinand Alexander Porsche** *(right)* **son of Ferry**

them twelve out of 16 rounds, duelling to the finish at Portugal for the driver's championship which Lauda won by just half a point, McLaren having easily secured the constructor's championship by mid-season. The following season, Prost levelled things up by coming home first in five rounds to take the driver's championship; Lauda managed just one first place, and McLaren took their second consecutive constructor's prize. For the 1986 season, Lauda's place was taken by Keke Rosberg, who did not have the best of seasons, his best

ABOVE RIGHT
Celebrations after the final Formula 1 round of 1984 in Estoril. From left to right John Barnard (Team Technical Director) Alain Prost, Ron Dennis (Commercial Director and Race Team Manager) and Niki Lauda. Marlboro McLaren had already secured the Constructor's Championship with Lauda's win at Monza, but Prost just failed to take the Driver's Championship from Lauda in the final round

RIGHT Lauda drives the McLaren during the 1985 Formula 1 season; that year he managed only one win, but Prost came home first in five rounds, to take the Driver's Championship. The Constructor's Title went once again to McLaren

LEFT The 1961 German Grand Prix at the Nürburgring. The 787s put in a poor performance in the first two races of the season at Monaco and Zandvoort. Porsche reinstated the 718, driven here by Dan Gurney of the USA, but there was to be no Formula 1 success that year

BELOW The Porsche 787 Formula 1, which was introduced in 1960, was based on the their successful Formula 2 718 and 718/2 cars

RIGHT **After several years out of Formula 1, Porsche joined forces with Footwork to make an assault on the 1990 to 1994 seasons. Everything started off well enough, but problems began to creep in as early as 1991. Footwork called a temporary halt to the relationship, but in fact the partnership was never reinstated**

BELOW RIGHT **Teo Fabi at the wheel of the Quaker State Porsche 2708 Indycar. Not the most successful of starts, and everyone concerned must have wondered if more good money had been thrown after bad**

LEFT **The 3.5 litre V12 engine produced by Porsche for the Footwork team**

result being a second at Monaco, but with everything down to the last race at Adelaide, Prost again took the title – by just two points from Williams' Nelson Piquet – and McLaren made it a hat-trick of Constructors' Championships beating Williams by just two and a half points.

But despite the successes, Porsche decided it would not, for the time being, remain involved in Formula One racing. In 1990, Porsche joined forces with the Footwork team to make another assault on Formula One. Porsche provided a new, 3.5 litre V12 engine, and Alan Jenkins of Footwork designed a new car, the FA12, to accommodate it – a promising start to what was intended to be a four-year partnership. The drivers were Italians Michele Alboreto and Alex Caffi, with Stefan Johansson backing them up. The plan was to make steady progress throughout the 1991 season, then use the winter months of the year for Footwork to perfect a second version of the car and for Porsche to reduce the weight and increase the power of the engine. But by midway through the 1991 season it was becoming obvious that all was not well. The car was neither reliable nor competitive

BELOW RIGHT **The P6B Racing Car designed by Porsche in 1979 to be run in the Indy races by the Interscope team and driven by Danny Ongais. A change in the rules caused the challange to be stillborn though – and a very costly exercise in both money and manpower it had been**

OPPOSITE **For the 1989 season, Porsche revamped the 2708 with a new chassis among other improvements. In its distinctive livery, the Quaker State Porsche 89P with Teo Fabi at the wheel came home first in the Mid-Ohio race**

enough. Conscious of the damaging effects of 'testing in public', Porsche and Footwork decided to call a temporary halt to the F! programme. From the French Grand Prix onwards, Footwork reverted to the Cosworth-engined cars of the previous season, and Porsche took their problems away to Weissach to solve without the interruption that race-pressures would bring. The intention was to re-instate the partnership before the end of the season, but in the event not enough progress was made to be sure of even moderate success, and Porsche decided to pull out of Formula One altogether.

Porsche's first assault on the Indianapolis 500 was announced in 1979; the following season would see Porsche racing a car designated P6B being run by the Interscope Racing Team. The engine, designated 935/76 was state of the art; air-cooled but with water-cooled cylinder heads. The driver was to be Danny Ongais, and everything was in place. Unfortunately for everyone concerned, the US Auto Club officials decided to limit pressure to 48psi – at which level the engine would be totally uncompetitive – and the challenge was off. Not that racing director Manfred Janke let it go without a fight,

but no compromise was reached, and all that was left was to count the cost in terms of money, time and manpower. It was not until 1986 that Porsche re-approached Indianapolis, with plans for a 2600 cc V8 engine on the drawing board. The 2708 Indycar was being tested at Weissach by the end of 1987 in preparation for the 1988 season, where the Quaker State sponsored Porsche would be making its debut, driven by Teo Fabi.

It was not an auspicious debut as it turned out, a wheel flying off the car in the pit lane, although Fabi was lying ninth when he exited, and was fortunately unhurt. Porsche felt that the 2708 was not up to scratch, so a March chassis was brought in as a replacement. Things improved slightly for the rest of the season, but there was no instant success story here. The season was overshadowed in October by the death of Al Holbert, whose light aircraft crashed while taking off. Porsche, in co-operation with March, set about planning for the 1989 season. Then it came right. Porsche Cars North America rejoiced as Teo Fabi, who had started from pole position, stormed home to take the Mid-Ohio race in the distinctive green and white Quaker State Porsche March 89P. The team dedicated the victory to the memory of Al Holbert.

Throughout the season, car, team and driver did well, but did not take the series. Unfortunately this success was not the start of a new Porsche racing dynasty. The 1990 season was frustrating for Porsche and the Indycar project fizzled out. Porsche had worked with March to build cars to enter the CART Championship, and John Andretti was ready to join Fabi in the team. But when the rules were clarified, it became clear that the designers would have to go back to the drawing board if they were going to produce anything that would qualify. It would all be too expensive and time consuming, and that was that.

CHAPTER SEVEN

ONE-MAKE RACING

uring the mid-eighties, one-manufacturer racing started to gain popularity in Europe. To appeal to this trend, Porsche introduced a new series in 1986, the Porsche 944 Turbo Cup. This was a series of six races, with all the cars prepared at Zuffenhausen and sold ready to race. The cars were powered by standard engines fitted with catalytic converters which produced 220hp. This was the first time that any manufacturer had run a series with cats fitted, and it provided an ideal proving ground to assess just what was possible under full load.

The first champion was Joachim Winkelhock. For 1987, the series was extended to ten races, with rounds in Italy and Belgium. The power was increased to 250 bhp, and the standard ABS braking system was compulsory. The 944 series was followed by the Carrera Cup Championships. Series were held in various countries, being particularly popular in Germany, France and Japan. The championships have gained a reputation for being close-run, often decided on the last race of the season. Many of the drivers too have had their careers launched by the Carrera series. Winners of the German series include Roland Asch in 1991, Uwe Alzen in '92, Wolfgang Land in '93 and Bernd Maylander in '94; in the French rounds, Jean-Pierre Malcher in '91, Dominique Dupuy in '92 and '93 and Christophe Bouchut in '94.

As part of the programme of celebration to mark the thirtieth anniversary of the 911 in 1993, the Porsche Supercup was launched. There were nine races in the series, seven of which took place on Grand Prix weekends and two supported the German Saloon Car Championship. Thirty identical Carrera 2s battled for supremacy, racing over 80 kms and accumulating points throughout the season. The first winner was Altfrid Heger, who took the

prize narrowly, beating contender Uwe Alzen in the last race of the season. VIP drivers were also invited to race. Motorcycle champion Kevin Schwantz, Formula One driver Mika Hakkinen and World Rally Champion Walter Roehrl took part in the first race, with Rally Champion Ari Vatanen, Chris Rea and Craig T Nelson taking the wheel for 1994. That year also saw the introduction of the grid lottery, which effectively meant that the fastest six drivers in practice would draw lots for the grid positions. A new car was introduced, the 911 Cup 3.8, which produced 310 bhp and weighed in at 1100 kg, and all the rounds were run as support races to the European rounds of the Grand Prix season. Once again, the winner was decided in the last race of the season, with

PREVIOUS PAGE
Supercup, 1995, a race series introduced in celebration of the 911's 30th birthday in 1993

LEFT **Roland Asch leads at the start of the Carrera 2 cup round at the Osterreichring in 1990**

BELOW LEFT
Competitors in the 1986 Porsche 944 Turbo Cup. Naturally this racing is extremely competitive, and once on the track, no mercy is shown. Off-track though, the Porsche races are friendly affairs, with very little of the breastbeating that can so easily spoil motorsport

RIGHT **The Porsche Supercup 1995. The season comprised nine rounds, each over a distance of about 80km, lasting about thirty minutes. Drivers accumulate points, not just from winning the races, but by being one of the four fastest in practice sessions too. Porsche define the car that can be used, and only this car is admissible. So for the 1995 year this car was designated Porsche 911 Cup 3.8, 1995**

ABOVE, CENTRE & BELOW RIGHT **The Pirelli classic offers yet another opportunity for non-professional racing drivers to compete at the top level of motorsport. One of the great strengths of Porsche's racing philosophy is that it encompasses motorsport at every level**

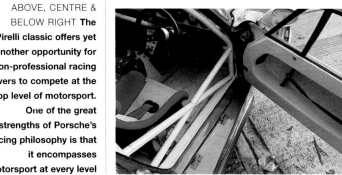

LEFT **The Supercup of 1995. All cars are fitted with safety equipment including roll cage. The angle of the rear wing is preset, gearboxes are sealed, the original suspension setup may not be changed ... in short, the Supercup contestants are on a level playing field, and driving ability counts for a great deal**

BELOW LEFT **The Porsche 911 Cup 3.8 Model Year 1996, as used for the Porsche Pirelli Supercup and National Carrera Cups. The 3746cc 6 cylinder boxer motor give 315bhp at 6,200. 0 to 100km/h (60mph) is in 4.7 seconds; top speed is 280km/h (168mph)**

Alzen victorious, just beating Emmanuel Collard and Jean-Pierre Malcher, who won the title, again in the last race, in 1995.

Celebrity drivers in the Pirelli-sponsored Supercup included Formula One stalwart Eddie Irvine and newcomer Ralf Schumacher. For the 1996 season, the 911 Cup 3.8 went to the start with further fine-tuning of the engine, suspension and gearbox by Weissach. The 3.8 litre flat

engine provided 315 bhp at 6,200 rpm, an increase largely due to new valve gear and other technical changes. The cars run on lead free fuel and use catalytic converters. The winner of the 1996 series was Frenchman Emmanuel Collard.

Such were the great successes of Porsche owners and drivers in various parts of the world that the company decided, in 1970, to award a cup and cash prizes to those who did the best job. The team and driver had to be genuinely independent of the factory, and points were awarded for results in international and national championships.

The first winner was Dutchman Gijs van Lennep driving for the Finnish Porsche importer and enthusiast Antti Wihuri, and the following year Cologne driver Erwin Kremer won the Porsche cup with a 911 which he prepared himself, helped by his brother Manfred.

ABOVE RIGHT & RIGHT
Wolfgang Land, the Porsche Carrera Cup winner of 1993, leads the field in his Roock Racing Team car, although the rest of the pack are not far behind; fresh air between tyre and tarmac is par for the course

After that, the Kremers concentrated more on team management and have won the Porsche Cup no fewer then 11 times in 27 years: John Fitzpatrick won overall in Kremer Porsches in 1972 and in 1974, Clemens Schickentanz in 1973, Bob Wollek in 1976, 1977, 1978 and again in 1981 – and Wollek won twice more in cars prepared by Reinhold Joest. Joest is the second most successful entrant having won nine times, but only once has the cup gone to America when Price Cobb won for the Kelly Moss team in 1994. There has been a female winner too, Swiss Lilian Bryner who shared the Porsche Cup with partner Enzo Calderari in 1995 after an outstanding season in their Stadler Motorsport Porsche Carrera RSR. The Porsche Cup is very seriously contested, not only for the great prestige of winning, but for a share of the DM300,000 prize fund awarded by Porsche AG.

WEISSACH

PREVIOUS PAGE
**Aerial view of the
Porsche development
and testing facility at
Weissach. Racing cars
are developed and
produced here, using
the latest technology
and methods**

The name of Weissach has, since the early 1970s, been synonymous with Porsche's excellence in engineering, consultancy, and in endurance racing. Tight security surrounds this great complex of modern offices, test houses, test track, a tank proving ground suitable only for NATO tanks (and Porsche's rally winners!) skid pads, noise and emission areas – this list goes on. There is almost no facet of automotive development that cannot be researched by Porsche at the Weissach centre, but the most visible face is the competitions headquarters directed, from 1995, by Herbert Ampferer.

Huschke von Hanstein created the competitions department in the 1950s, taking charge of race administration, signing of drivers, such contracts as there were with oil and tyre companies, negotiating with organisers and not least conducting Porsche's public relations with considerable flair.

Ferdinand Piech, appointed Head of Research and development in 1965, felt increasingly that competitions were *his* domain and sought to curtail von Hanstein's range of influence. By the end of 1968 the aristocratic Von Hanstein decided to move on to the newly created VW-Porsche concern in Ludwigsburg, and was succeeded by Rico Steinemann. It was Steinemann, a Swiss who had to negotiate tough terms with the ACO and the FIA over the infamous moving tail flaps at Le Mans in 1969, threatening to withdraw the entire works team unless they kept the mobile flaps as an aid to safety. He won!

Piech left Porsche's employment in 1971, a time when Professor Porsche felt that nepotism had gone far enough and asked all his sons and nephews to look elsewhere. Dipl.Ing. Helmuth Bott became director of research and development at Weissach, while in Zuffenhausen Manfred Jantke was appointed head of public

relations and competitions director. The separation of offices underlined the functions as Jantke continued to look after contracts and general policies, while the cars were prepared and tactics controlled by various engineers at Weissach. Peter Falk was the first officially appointed Competitions Director from 1982-1990, in charge of the 956 and 962 programmes, succeeded by Swiss Max Weitl (1990-95) and then by Herbert Ampferer.

Hans Mezger was head of race engine development until 1991, succeeded by Herbert Ampferer, who combines his race director duties with supervising competitions

powertrain development and Ing. Norbert Singer has made a wonderful career out of developing the 911 model for competitions, from 1972 to the present time.

The current Porsche GT1 model, which won the 24-hours of le Mans on its debut in 1996, came 24 years after Singer and Mezger started work on the Porsche 911 Carrera RSR, which won the 24-Hours of Daytona in 1973.

It was followed by the Martini-liveried RSR turbo in 1974, the 934, 935 and 936 which swept their opponents aside in 1976, the omnipotent 956 and 962 models which dominated Group C and IMSA Championships racing between 1982 and 1988 – mention should be made here of Ing. Horst Reitter, the chassis engineer responsible for the Group C cars and their successors – the cheeky Dauer Porsche 962 LM which was introduced to the Grand Touring category, the GT2 model and its GT1 class Evolution, and then the GT1 itself, another of Porsche's timeless classics.

To backtrack to the very beginning of the Weissach phenomenon, In the early years of Porsche sportscar production, there was little problem using stretches of public road for testing. There were few cars, and the excellent autobahn from Stuttgart to Heilbron was almost always deserted, and doubled as a handy test track. But as traffic increased, this became more difficult, especially the extreme testing required for racing cars. From 1953, a small aerodrome near Malmsheim was made available but it had neither the space nor the scope to offer a long term solution. It became obvious that the only answer was to establish an in-house testing centre with purpose-built areas simulating every conceivable road condition and track situation. A piece of land was found between the villages of Weissach and Flacht, 25 km west of Stuttgart. The site had one great advantage: out in the country, it was well away from public view.

Once the initial planning was done, everything moved fast. By the end of 1960, Porsche had received exemption from land protection regulations and finalised the purchase of 309 acres from 125 different land owners. One year later, Dr Ferry Porsche had ceremonially cut the first turf, another year on and the skid pad and roads were ready for use. Porsche's development division, which was expanding all the time, was still at Stuttgart at this time, but there

RIGHT **The Weissach wind tunnel has been used to test not just motor cars but also products with no automotive connections – the aerodynamic properties of the humble football have been tested out here as well as the latest Porsche racers. (Thus confirming the editor's darkest suspicions concerning the European Championships, 1996)**

was no scope at all for growth on that site. Construction of the new development centre at Weissach began early in 1969, and in the summer of 1971 the development division started to move into their new headquarters, which was officially opened on October 1st that year. In August 1982, the Racing and Sportscar Division was established – a separate entity within the Weissach complex.

Every car for competition is checked very thoroughly at Weissach, going through a variety of tests, including a 1000 km run over a special bumpy surface. One of the points to this is that the car should, if it leaves the race track, be able to drive over any of the infield surfaces without damage to the suspension.

This procedure has been missed only once in the past 25 years; there was a huge snowstorm at Weissach, making testing impossible, and it may not be entirely coincidence that each of the three 908 Spyders that missed their trials retired from their race at Sebring with broken frame or suspension parts.

Today, the Weissach centre co-ordinates all Porsche's research and development projects, employing more than 25% of the total workforce, and covering over 672,000 sq m, including three test tracks and specialised testing areas. Not all the work done here is for Porsche; 40% of research done here is for external clients, some automotive, but by no means all. Safety and environmental issues

RIGHT The team photo of 1969 from left to right; Bjorn Waldegaard, Hans Hermann, Pauli Toivonen, Rico Steinemann, Rolf Stommelen, Kurt Ahrens, Udo Schutz, Brian Redman, Dick Attwood, Gerard Larrousse, Jo Siffert and Gerhard Mitter

BELOW RIGHT & FAR RIGHT
The Porsche Museum at Zuffenhausen where the history of Porsche from the very earlist days can be traced. Examples of the famous racers and production cars are all here in 'in the flesh' There is also a wealth of information to be studied on Porsche, the company and the cars, plus posters and photographs of Porsche milestones through the years

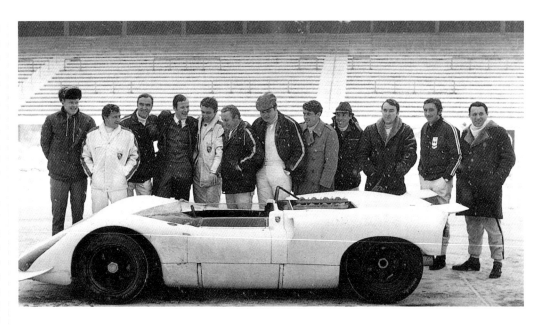

have come to the forefront over the past few years, Porsche being one of the European manufacturers to work on the joint 'Prometheus' research project, aiming to find solutions to the problems of traffic flow, environmental damage, safety and economy. As a self contained operation, the work at Weissach is based on the principle that a project team supplies all the information and know-how for every aspect of a vehicle's design and development. By having every facility in one place, simultaneous research and development processes complement each other.

These processes are amazingly varied, with workshops for machining, plastics-processing, assembly techniques and painting. Engine testing rigs, air and liquid flow labs,

LEFT As part of Porsche's high-speed endurance programme, this 928S achieved 3749 miles in 24 hours at the Nardo test track on 20th/21st November 1982. The drivers were Gerhard Plattner, Peter Zbinden and Peter Lovett. The average speed over the test was 156.22mph

RIGHT **At the
Zuffenhausen Museum –
a V12 engine open for
inspection. Its sheer size
makes one wonder how
it could ever be
shoehorned into a car of
any kind, and gives some
inkling of the technical
complexity that building
a racing machine entails**

roller dynamometers, flywheel test rigs, acoustic measuring chambers too, with impressive full-size and quarter-scale wind tunnels, climatic chambers and full crash-testing facilities. Porsche say that the development centre will never be complete; it will change constantly, adapting to meet their needs and incorporating new technologies and new expectations.

THE ULTIMATE TEST OF ENDURANCE?

Here is one example of what the Weissach engineers get up to, (though not strictly concerning the competition department, who are, as may be imagined, fairly reticent around authors and journalists) and it's also not a day-to-day project, owing quite a lot to the input of the Porsche publicity department. On 22nd January 1992, a very special endurance test began at the Weissach Development Centre. The intention was to take a Porsche 968 across three continents, allowing the car to experience extreme driving conditions that would push it to its limits. From this exercise an enormous amount of data would be collected and analysed and the conclusions would have a profound effect on the future development of Porsche engines, both the road-going and the racing varieties. The aim was to cover 100,000 km in 100 days, but this was no arbitrary mad dash – everything had been meticulously planned to incorporate terrain and conditions simulating the equivalent of five car-lives of wear. The chief driver chosen for this test was Gerhard Plattner, who was no stranger to feats of endurance. He held the record for driving around the world – in 28 days and 16 hours – and would notch up his two-millionth kilometre during the test.

The marathon test took place in several parts. One major milestone was the first drive of a sportscar with catalytic converter through the desert in Morocco and across the atrocious roads of the Atlas Mountains. Then there was an economy test. Using just one tank of fuel, the car was driven by guest driver Karl

LEFT Development, testing, then testing and more testing; the Weissach engineers prepare cars for the 1987 season

BELOW LEFT Gerhard Plattner was often to be found driving cars a very long way for a very long time in the name of endurance testing. Here he comes to the end of a 100,000km test in the 911 Carrera 4 in 1995. Development Director Horst Marchant wields the chequered flag

Habsburg-Lothringen, (grandson of the last Austrian Emperor), between the most westerly and the most easterly capitals of the former Austo-Hungarian Empire, Innsbruck and Budapest. Next came 24 hours on Germany's 963 km A7 Autobahn. Plattner and his team drove its length three times. Although speed-restrictions were meticulously observed, and refuelling stops included, the average speed for this part of the test was still 120 kmh. The next section provided the only major disap-pointment of the test. The plan was for a 24-hour drive over the 17 km road between the Sellajoch and Grodnerjoch mountain passes, which would have meant a total altitude change of 56 km, but the whole stage had to be abandoned. The passes had been closed due to extreme conditions and the imminent danger of an avalanche.

The test then moved to North America, and started with a drive across the ice from Inuvik to Tuktoyaktuk, 200 km further north on Mackenzie bay. This remote Eskimo settle-ment can only be reached by a land route – an ice route in truth – from December to April, when the minus 37°C temperatures ensure a firm base. After a journey down the Alaska Highway and across Yellowstone Park, there followed several hours on the Bonneville Salt Flats race track. This part of the journey ended at the most southerly point of the US, Key West in Florida, where the temperature mea-sured 26°C – a 63 degree change. The final part of the test took place on Italy's Nardo test track, where 5566 km were covered in 24 hours at full throttle, with only the briefest of stops for refuelling and visual checks. The last of the 100,000 km was recorded on the jour-ney back to Cologne, where the marathon ended at the television studio. For everyone involved, the real satisfaction of it all came later, when the car had been returned to Weissach and tested, then stripped down and inspected in minute detail. There were no parts in need of replacement: in fact the only repair during the whole trip had been a broken tank lid. It had been a good test, good for morale and good for public relations, and first-class data had been collected for future research and development.

PORSCHE MOTORSPORT NORTH AMERICA

Porsche Motorsport North America (PMNA) with its headquarters in Warrington, Pennsylvania, was created in 1985. It took over from the Porsche Racing Service, which had operated since the 1972 Can-Am project as Porsche AG's racing support group. After Porsche Cars North America was established, Porsche founded PMNA and chose veteran racing driver Al Holbert to head the new divi-sion, a subsidiary of Porsche AG. The aim of PMNA was to provide racing support of all kinds throughout America, encouraging both teams and drivers to enter competition and to win races. This support comes in the form of technical expertise, advice, logistical planning and financial backing. The support team answer questions and solve problems, and they also supply complete cars ready to race, either directly from Weissach, or by the assembling of imported components.

They provide a race-track parts depart-ment in the shape of a giant 48-foot trailer with space for over 30,000 racing parts, large and small. PMNA sponsors the Porsche Cup North America Series, which is open to both amateur and professional drivers. They also provide awards to Porsche teams competing in the pro SCCA/Escort Endurance Showroom Stock series, IMSA's Firestone Firehawk Street Stock pro series, and the SCCA's amateur National Divisional Championship. In addition, the Porsche Meister Team Cup is awarded to

the IMSA Camel GT Porsche team best representing the company in terms of performance, appearance, co-operation and attitude. In 1997, Alwyn Springer was officially appointed Director of Motorsport in North America, a job he had been doing in reality for some years.

The importance of Porsche competition efforts in North America should not be overshadowed by Le Mans glories. Almost half the 81 car grid for the Rolex 24 at Daytona in February 1997 was made by Porsche in Stuttgart and although even the leading Porsches stood little chance of winning the race – a result of rule changes which favoured the World Sports Car entries and were biased against turbocharged engines – the legions of private owners were not deterred.

Porsche has won the Daytona 24 hours on no fewer than 19 occasions since it was first run in 1985, and the Sebring 12 Hours on 17 occasions. Incredibly, Porsche was unbeaten at Sebring between 1976 and 1988, a run of 13 successive victories that spanned the Porsche 911 Carrera RSR, the Group 4 934, the Group 5 935, and then the IMSA GTP

dominating 962 model that ruled the roost between 1985 and 1988. Of course Porsche was successful everywhere in North America, but Florida has been the manufacturer's main hunting ground: Daytona in February, Sebring in March and Palm Beach, too, in years gone by. Hurley Haywood, a Florida resident, is Porsche's most successful endurance driver, edging out Jacky Ickx and Derek Bell by virtue of his great successes at home. Haywood, still an active driver and a potential winner, famously won the Daytone 24 Hours in 1973 in company with Peter Gregg driving the brand new Porsche 911 Carrera RSR.

Haywood became the first man to win the 24 Hours of Daytona and Le Mans in one season, 1977, and his endurance crown consists of five overall wins at Daytona, three at Le Mans and two at Sebring.

Al Holbert and Derek Bell established a unique record in winning the 24 Hours of Daytona and Le Mans both in 1986 and again in 1987, four successive round-the-clock victories, or, to put it another way, 96 Hours unbeaten in the Porsche 962 model.

APPENDICES

LE MANS OVERALL AND MAJOR CLASS VICTORIES

Year	Class	Drivers
1951	1100cc	Veuillet/Mouche
1952	1100cc	Veuillet/Mouche
1953	1500cc sports	von Frankenberg/Frere
	1500cc sports	Glockler/Herrmann
1954	1500cc	Claes/Stasse
	1100cc	Duntov/Oliver
1955	1500cc	Polenski/von Frankenberg
	1100cc	Duntov/Veuillet
1956	1500cc sports	von Frankenberg/von Tripps
1957	1500cc sports	Hugus/de Beaufort
1960	1600cc sports	Barth/Seidel
	1600cc GT	Linge/Walter
1962	1600cc	Barth/Herrmann
1963	2000cc	Barth/Linge
1964	2000cc GT	Buchet/Ligier
1965	2000cc proto	Linge/Nocker
	2000cc GT	Koch/Fischaber
1966	2000cc proto	Siffert/Davis
	2000cc sports	Klass/Stommelen
1967	sports overall	Elford/Pon
	2000cc GT	Buchet/Linge
	2000cc proto	Siffert/Herrmann
1968	group 3	Gaban/Vanderschrick
1969	group 6	Herrmann/Larrousse
	group 3	Gaban/Deprez
1970	overall (917K)	Herrmann/Attwood
	group 6	Marko/Lins
	group 4	Chasseuil/Ballot-Lena
1971	overall (917K)	Marko/van Lennep
	group 6	Brun/Mattli
	group 4	Tourol/Anselme
1975	group 4	Fitzpatrick/van Lennep/Schurti
1976	overall (936)	Ickx/van Lennep/Hezemans
1977	overall (936)	Ickx/Haywood/Barth
1978	IMSA	Redman/Barbour
	group 4	Busby/Cord/Knoop
1979	overall (935 K/3)	Ludwig/Whittington/ Whittington
	IMSA	Stommelen/Barbour/Newman
	group 4	Muller/Pallavacini/Vanoli
1980	IMSA	Fitzpatrick/Redman/Barbour
	group 5	Schornstein/Grohs/Tscirnhaus
1981	overall (936/81)	Ickx/Bell
	group 5	Cooper/Wood/Bourgoignie
	group 4	Bertapelle/Perrier/Salam
	IMSA GTO	Schurti/Rouse
1982	overall (956)	Ickx/Bell
	group 5	Cooper/Smith/Bourgoignie
	group 4	Cleare/Dron/Jones
	GTX	Fitzpatrick/Hobbs
1983	overall (956)	Haywood/Holbert/Schuppan
1984	overall (956 Joest)	Pescarolo/Ludwig
1985	overall (956 B Joest)	Ludwig/Barilla/Winter
1986	overall (962 C)	Stuck/Bell/Holbert
1987	overall (962 C)	Stuck/Bell/Holbert
1994	overall (Dauer 962)	Dalmas/Baldi/Haywood
1996	overall (Joest-Porsche WSC95)	Reuter/Jones/Wurz
	GT1	Stuck/Boutsen/Wollek
1997	overall (Joest TWR)	Alboreto/Johansson/Kristensen

MILLE MIGLIA

Year	Class	Drivers
1952	1500cc	Berckheim/Lurani
	1100cc	Metternich/Einseidel
1953	1300cc sports	von Hoesch/Engel
	1500cc sports	Herrmann/Bauer
1954	1600cc	von Frankenberg/Sauter
	1500cc sports	Herrmann/Linge
1955	1500cc sports	Seidel
	1300cc GT	von Frankenberg
1956	1300cc GT	Strahle
	1600cc GT	Persson/Lundquist
1957	1500cc sports	Maglioli
	1600cc GT	Strahle/Linge

TARGA FLORIO

Year	Class	Drivers
1956	overall (1500cc)	Maglioli
1958	1500cc sports	Behra/Scarlatti
	1600cc GT	von Hanstein/Pucci
1959	overall	Barth/Seidel
	2600cc GT	von Hanstein/Pucci
1960	overall	Bonnier/Herrmann
	1600cc sports	Barth/Hill
	2000cc sports	Bonnier/Herrmann
1961	sports	Bonnier/Gurney
1962	1600cc GT	Herrmann/Linge
	2000cc proto	Bonnier/Vaccarella
1963	overall proto	Bonnier/Abate
	overall GT (2000cc)	Barth/Linge
	1600cc GT	Koch/Schroter
1964	overall (2000cc GT)	Pucci/Davis
	protos	Barth/Maglioi
1965	2000cc proto	Mitter/Davis
	2000cc GT	Klass/Pucci
1966	overall (2000cc sp)	Mairesse/Muller
	1600cc GT	Tarenghi/Pardi
1967	overall	Stommelen/Hawkins
	(+2000cc proto)	
	2000cc proto	Cella/Biscaldi
1968	overall	Elford/Maglioli
	sports	von Wendt/Kaussen
	GT	Haldi/Greub
1969	overall	Mitter/Schutz
	group 3	Ostine/Nomex
1970	overall	Siffert/Redman
1971	group 4	Cheneviere/Keller
1972	group 4	Pica/Gottifredi
1973	overall	Muller/van Lennep

MONTE CARLO RALLY

Year	Class	Drivers
1956	1300cc GT	Gacon/Arcan
1962	1600cc GT	Isenbugel/Springer
1964	2000cc GT	Klass/Wencher
1965	2000cc GT	Bohringer/Wutherich
1967	GT	Elford/Stone
1968	overall (GT)	Elford/Stone
1969	overall	Waldegaard/Helmer
1970	overall	Waldegaard/Helmer
1978	overall	Nicolas/Laverne

SEBRING 12 HOUR RACE

Year	Class	Drivers
1955	1600cc	von Hanstein/Linge
	1300cc sports	Brundage/Fowler
	1100cc sports	O'Shea/Koster
1957	sports	Bunker/Wallace
1958	1600cc GT	von Hanstein/Linge
	2000cc sports	von Trips/Bonnier
	1600cc GT	von Hanstein/de Beaufort
1960	overall (1600cc sport)	Gendebien/Herrmann
	2000cc GT	Sheppard/Dungan
1961	sports	Holbert/Penske
1963	2000cc GT	Holbert/Wester
	1600cc GT	Cassel/Sesslar
1964	2000cc proto	Cunningham/Underwood
	2000cc GT	Pon/Buzzetta
1966	2000cc proto	Herrmann/Buzzetta/Mitter
	2000cc sports	Follmer/Gregg
	2000cc GT	Ryan/Coleman
1967	2000cc proto	Mitter/Patrick
	overall (GT)	Kirby/Johnson
1968	overall	Siffert/Herrmann
1969	group 3	Wicky/Sage/Larrousse
1970	group 6	McQueen/Revson
1971	overall	Elford/Larrousse
	group 4 2000cc	Locke/Everett
1972	group 4	Gregg/Haywood

from 1976 IMSA (Camel) GT Championship winners

1976	Holbert/Keyser
1977	Dyer/Frisselle
1978	Redman/Mendez/Garretson
1979	Akin/McFarlin/Woods
1980	FitzPatrick/Barbour
1981	Haywood/Holbert/Leven
1982	Paul/Paul
1983	Baker/Mullen/Nierop
1985	Wollek/Foyt
1986	Akin/Stuck/Gartner
1987	Mass/Rahal
1988	Ludwig/Stuck

DAYTONA RACES

1959	overall	van Dory/Mieres
1962	sports	Ryan
1963	2000cc GT	von Hanstein
	2000cc GT	Bonnier
1965	2000cc GT	Kolb/Heftler
1966	2000cc sorts	Mitter/Buzzetta
	2000cc proto	Herrmann/Linge
1967	2000cc proto	Herrmann/Siffert
1968	overall (proto)	Elford/Neerpasch/Siffert/
		Stommelen/Herrmann
	Touring	Gregg/Axelsson
	GT	Hanrioud/Garant
1969	group 3	Jennings/Wetson/Adamowicz
1970	overall	Rodriguez/Kinnunen
	group 42000cc	Wright/Bean/Meaney
1971	overall	Rodriguez/Oliver
	group 4 2000cc	Duval/Nicholas/Bailey

1972	group 4		Gregg/Haywood

from 1973 World Championship of Makes winners (24 hour)
and IMSA (Camel) GT Championship winners (250)

1973	24 hour	Gregg/Haywood
1975	24 hour	Gregg/Haywood
1977	24 hour	Graves/Haywood/Helmick
	250	Dyer
1978	24 hour	Stommelen/Gregg/Hezemans
	250 – I	Gregg
	250 – II	Gregg
1979	24 hour	Ongais/Haywood/Field
	250 – I	Haywood/Mendez
	250 – II	Whittington (B)
1980	24 hour	Stommelen/Joest/Merl
	250 – I	Fitzpatrick
	250 – II	Joest/Moretti
1981	24 hour	Redman/Rahal/Garretson
	250 – I	Haywood/de Narvaez
	250 – II	Paul

from 1982 IMSA Camel GT Championship winners

1982	24 hour	Paul/Paul/Stommelen
1983	24 hour	Henn/Wollek/Ballot-Lena/Foyt
	250	Haywood/Foyt
1984	24 hour	van der Merwe/Martin/Duxbury
	3 hour	Holbert/Bell
1985	24 hour	Foyt/Wollek/Unser Sn/Boutsen
	3 hour	Holbert/Unser Jn
1986	24 hour	Holbert/Bell/Unser Jn
1987	24 hour	Holbert/Bell/Unser Jn/Robinson
1989	24 hour	Wollek/Bell/Andretti(J)
1991	24 hour	Winter/Jelinski/Pescarolo/Haywood/Wollek
1995	24 hour	Lässig/Bouchut/Lavaggi/Werner

LEFT **Keith Martin of Brian Currie Ltd, based in the UK, drives a 1971 2700cc Dulon Porsche in the Supersports class race at the Nürburgring Oldtimer event of 1995**

550 Spyder
Year 1953-55
Capacity 1498cc
Cylinders 4
BHP/RPM 110/6200
Wheelbase 82.8
Length 141.8
Width 61
Weight 1512

RS Spyder
Year 1956
Capacity 1498cc
Cylinders 4
BHP/RPM 135/7200
Wheelbase 82.8
Length 149.5
Width 63.8
Weight 1301

RSK 718 1500, 1600
Year 1957, 1958
Capacity 1498cc,
1588cc
Cylinders 4
BHP/RPM 142/7500
165/8000
Wheelbase 82.8
Length 149.8
Width 58.3
Weight 1146, 1148

RS60, RS61
Year 1960, 1961
Capacity 1588cc
Cylinders 4
BHP/RPM 165/8000
Wheelbase 82.8
Length 149.8
Width 57.8
Weight 1058

904 GTS
Year 1964
Capacity 1966cc
Cylinders 4
BHP/RPM 180/7000
Wheelbase 90.8
Length 162
Width 60.8
Weight 1433

906 (Carrera 6)
Year 1966
Capacity 1991cc
Cylinders 6
BHP/RPM 210/8000
Wheelbase 90.5
Length 162
Width 66.1
Weight 1235

910/6
Year 1967
Capacity 1991cc
Cylinders 6
BHP/RPM 220/8000
Wheelbase 90.5
Length 162
Width 66.1
Weight 1268

907/6
Year 1967
Capacity 1991cc
Cylinders 6
BHP/RPM 220/8000
Wheelbase 90.5
Length 158.8
Width 67.8
Weight 1260

908
Year 1968
Capacity 2997cc
Cylinders 8
BHP/RPM 350/8400
Wheelbase 90.6
Length 192.5
Width 72
Weight 1452

909 Berg
Year 1968
Capacity 1981cc
Cylinders 8
BHP/RPM 275/9000
Wheelbase 89.3
Length 136
Width 70.8
Weight 947

917 Kurz (Lang)
Year 1969
Capacity 4494cc
Cylinders 12
BHP/RPM 520/8000
Wheelbase 90.6
Length 168.9 (188.2)
Width 74
Weight 1320 (1972)

911 RSR
Year 1973
Capacity 2806cc
Cylinders 6
BHP/RPM 315/8000
Wheelbase 89.4
Length 163.2
Width 73.8
Weight 2040

934
Year 1976
Capacity 2993cc
Cylinders 6
BHP/RPM 485/7000
Wheelbase 89.4
Length 165.3
Width 73.6
Weight 2470

935
Year 1976
Capacity 2856cc
Cylinders 6
BHP/RPM 590/7900
Wheelbase 89.4
Length 183.3
Width 78.6
Weight 2139

936
Year 1976
Capacity 2142cc
Cylinders 6
BHP/RPM 520/8000
Wheelbase 94.5
Length 165.3
Width 77.9
Weight 1588

P6B Indy
Year 1980
Capacity 21650cc
Cylinders 6
BHP/RPM 630/9000
Wheelbase 104.5
Length 179.0
Width -
Weight 1499

956
Year 1983
Capacity 2650CC
Cylinders 6
BHP/RPM 640/8000
Wheelbase 104.3
Length 189.0
Width 78.7
Weight 1797

962
Year 1984
Capacity 2856cc
Cylinders 6
BHP/RPM 650/8000
Wheelbase 109.1
Length 189.0
Width 78.7
Weight 1874

962C
Year 1985
Capacity 2649cc
Cylinders 6
BHP/RPM 630/8000
Wheelbase 109.1
Length 189.0
Width 78.7
Weight 1874

961
Year 1986
Capacity 2857cc
Cylinders 6
BHP/RPM 680/7800
Wheelbase 90.9
Length 172.4
Width 74.4
Weight 2921

2708 Indy
Year 1988
Capacity 2649cc
Cylinders 8
BHP/RPM 740/11200
Wheelbase 110.2
Length 183.5
Width 79.1
Weight 1550

962C
Year 1990
Capacity 3164cc
Cylinders 6
BHP/RPM 670/8300
Wheelbase 109.1
Length 189.0
Width 78.7
Weight 1980

90P CART
Year 1990
Capacity 2649cc
Cylinders 8
BHP/RPM 735/12000
Wheelbase 112.2
Length 184.9
Width 79.1
Weight 1550

911 GT1
Year 1995
Capacity 3200cc
Cylinders 6
BHP/RPM 600/7200
Height 46.2
Length 185.4
Width 77.9
Weight 2315

356
Year 1950
Capacity 1086cc
Cylinders 4
BHP/RPM 40/4200
Wheelbase 82.7
Length 155.6
Width 65.4
Weight 1829

911
Year 1965
Capacity 1991cc
Cylinders 6
BHP/RPM 130/6100
Wheelbase 87
Length 164
Width 63.4
Weight 2376

912
Year 1965
Capacity 1582cc
Cylinders 4
BHP/RPM 90/5800
Wheelbase 87
Length 164
Width 63.4
Weight 2134

914
Year 1969
Capacity 1679cc
Cylinders 4
BHP/RPM 80/5000
Wheelbase 96.5
Length 157
Width 65
Weight 1984

911 Carrera
Year 1972
Capacity 2687cc
Cylinders 6
BHP/RPM 210/6300
Wheelbase 89.3
Length 164
Width 65.4
Weight 2085

924
Year 1975
Capacity 1984cc
Cylinders 4
BHP/RPM 125/5800
Wheelbase 94.5
Length 166
Width 66
Weight 2592

928
Year 1977
Capacity 4474cc
Cylinders 8
BHP/RPM 240/5500
Wheelbase 98.4
Length 175.7
Width 72.3
Weight 3151

944
Year 1985
Capacity 2479
Cylinders 4
BHP/RPM 163/5800
Wheelbase 94.5
Length 166
Width 68.3
Weight 2635

959
Year 1987
Capacity 2857cc
Cylinders 6
BHP/RPM 450/6500
Wheelbase 89.4
Length 167.7
Width 72.4
Weight 3197

968
Year 1991
Capacity 2990cc
Cylinders 4
BHP/RPM 240/6200
Wheelbase 94 5
Length 170
Width 68.3
Weight 3144

911 Carrera
Year 1998
Capacity 3500
Cylinders 6
BHP (SAE net) 295
Wheelbase 94.1
Length 175.4
Width 69.7
Weight 3000